BOOM TOWN REFLECTIONS

VOLUME – 8

THE LONG ROAD HOME

By

Mark A. Gregg

An Imprint of Collins Publishing House

4900 California Ave, Bakersfield, CA 93309, USA

Collins's website address: www.collinspublishinghouse.com

First published in English by Collins Publishing House in 2024

1st Edition 2024

Mark A. Gregg © 2024

Mark A. Gregg asserts the moral right

to be identified as the author of this work.

A catalogue record for this book is available

from the Library of Congress United States.

LCCN: 2024925409

E Book ISBN: 978-1-966029-47-2

Paperback ISBN: 978-1-966029-48-9

Hardcover ISBN: 978-1-966029-49-6

Printed and bounded in United States of America.

For permission requests, contact
info@collinspublishinghouse.com!

Table Of Contents

CHAPTER 1
DES MOINES, IA

After totally destroying my career at the Bonanza Power Plant in Vernal, Utah, we were forced to start all over again due to an unbridled ego. I spastically jumped into the first thing presented to me. I was to become a contract, cogeneration plant, start-up engineer for Burns and McDonnell Engineering.

While I hadn't actually commissioned a cogeneration plant before, I had driven by one on the freeway. I mean, come on, how much did you need to know? Added to this was the incredible stress of leaving an 'umbilical cord' job with every conceivable benefit.

Working directly for the electric utilities was akin to being connected to a life-giving umbilical cord. If you were slightly motivated and stayed out of major trouble, the job would normally be a lifetime of employment security. This was something every man with a wife and three young children needed.

I was 30 years old and already worked for 6 different power companies (one of them twice) and one consulting firm. I was leaving all the amazing pay and benefits of a power plant supervisory job for what? Self-employment? Self-employment offering a paycheck only, no benefits, no insurance, no time-off, and no security. ***How could this be problematic?***

Looking back, it made no sense. In fact, it didn't make sense then. Unfortunately, a crushed ego and the realization you have become a major ***weasel*** becomes hard to digest. It

1

certainly warranted a substantial change. *A change that my amazing wife Vangie and our three kids were forced to endure with me.*

Immediately upon arriving in Des Moines, there was intense pressure on us. Burns and McDonnell Engineering wanted me in Mankato, Minnesota, ASAP. We had to find a place to live in a foreboding city we had never seen before. You could cut the tension between Vangie and me with a knife. Most of our previous moves were handled by the company that hired me. This move was handled entirely by us.

Because there wasn't a paid house hunting trip, we simply packed up the house in Vernal and the moving company hauled everything to Des Moines without us having the slightest clue where we would put it. Even worse, the entire moving process started on a *horrible* note.

During the loading process in Vernal, a large, very heavy, decorative brass swan hanging on the wall in the entryway to our split-entry house fell off the wall and stabbed one of the movers in in the upper right side of his torso. There was blood everywhere. It looked like we butchered a hog in the entryway of the house. He went partially into shock and just stood there bleeding profusely until Vangie jumped into action.

She immediately packed a couple of large bath towels around his upper torso and rushed him to the emergency room at the hospital. It took several dozen stitches to close up the deep and massive gash. He was unable to continue loading so we had to wait for someone to come from Salt Lake City to help finish the process, throwing us off by a day. Time was a sinister and unforgiving nemesis. As a contractor, every day I

2

didn't work was a day without income. Sadly, my indoctrination into 'contract' work was just beginning.

Our unceremonious arrival in Des Moines was on a dreary, steel-gray day. We chose an older Holiday Inn on Fleur Drive as our initial "command center," immediately enlisting a local real estate agency to help us find a suitable place to live. After three very strained and taut days of looking at places to rent, our nerves were frayed, and we were doing our best to not openly squabble in front of the kids.

Luckily, the kids were handling our stress extremely well. Brandi was 10, Brittanie was 7, and Josh was 4. The 1987-1988 school year had already begun but we couldn't put them in school until we found a place to live and knew what school they would attend.

Besides using the real estate rental agency, I was searching the Des Moines Register newspaper (classified ad section) for homes to rent. On our third day, I found an ad for a 3 bedroom, 3 bath, 1650 Sq Ft "executive home" located at 3530 SW 28th Street. The rent was $750.00 per month. This was quite pricy at the time, but we looked at it anyway.

We were required to pay the first and last month's rent and a $750.00 damage deposit. I probably could have **purchased** a house with this much money tied up in the rental.

Many years after our move to Des Moines, Vangie and I were talking about our lives together. She dropped a bomb on me that forever changed my life. She told me that she truly *"hated me"* during our time together in Des Moines. She said she felt trapped in a non-functional marriage a million miles away from everyone and everything she knew and held dear.

Looking back, it was easy to see why this was the case. I made my first stupendous mistake (of many to come) on our 5th day in Des Moines.

The moving truck rumbled to the front of our new home. The large, smelly, somewhat grimy movers put the ramps on the semi-trailer and began unloading our furniture and household goods. Did I supervise the unloading process and protect my vulnerable wife and three children? Sadly, and inexcusably, *No, I didn't.* To this very day, I honestly can't fathom what I was thinking or where my mind was.

About an hour into the unloading process, it appeared everything was going well enough that it was okay to leave for Mankato to start the new job. Yes, I was married to an angel. She told me I was lucky she was still there when I came home at the end of the next week.

The trip to Mankato from the new house in Des Moines took about 4 hours. I prayed much of the way. *How ironic.* I prayed for many things on that drive to Mankato but prayed primarily that things would go smoothly for Vangie. *Yet, I didn't stay and help her.* **Could I have been any more stupid or selfish? Probably, *but it is hard to imagine how.***

CHAPTER 2
MANKATO, MN

It wasn't difficult to find the plant in Mankato. It was a large industrial complex with grain elevators. Oddly, my life for the next several months was going to be surrounded by towering grain elevators. Armour, Gordan, & Miller's (AGM) entire universe was agriculture and grain processing. They produced oils, corn syrups, cereal, ethanol, and food products in general.

I quickly came to understand that **my** universe ~ **_power generation_** ~ was barely a blip on their radar. AGM was, firstly, a money machine and secondly, a grain milling company. Their only view of the power production process was a cost reduction to the grain milling operation that, ultimately, made them more money.

I was incredibly *underwhelmed* as I drove by my new plant. I was accustomed to massively large power plants, all with 600' tall (or greater) formidable concrete stacks. The cogeneration plant appeared to be a small, odd-shaped metal building with a gaunt, maybe 80' chimney. I'm not sure you could call it a stack. If size matters, this place doesn't matter. In fact, had it not been for the diminutive stack, it looked more like a small warehouse than a power plant.

The cooling tower was the size of a single-car garage. This, of course, made sense because their minuscule steam turbine was non-condensing. The cooling tower was only for plant equipment cooling, nothing more. After viewing the unimpressive, underwhelming facility, I drove back to the motel and went to bed, sleeping fitfully in anticipation of starting work the next morning.

Arriving at the plant early the following morning, the security guard at the front gate sent me to the parking lot of the Cogen plant. I was supposed to meet Rick Crown, the Plant Superintendent, in the control room. The entire plant was barely two stories tall except for the boiler, which had a little extra height on it. I was accustomed to 14 or more floors in a plant.

I walked inside and quickly looked around before trying to find the control room. It only took a few minutes to see the entire first floor, where most of the equipment was. This plant seemed little more than a small warehouse with random small equipment strewn haphazardly about.

Finding a narrow, dark stairwell, I climbed to the insignificant, poorly lit turbine deck… *If you could call it that.* It was a paltry, tight room with a turbine and generator about the size of a pick-up truck sitting on the floor.

The generator was the size of an electric boiler feed pump motor at a *real* power plant. There was one steam line into the turbine and one much larger line on the exhaust of the turbine. This was because it was a non-condensing turbine. The steam entered at 1200 psig and 950° and exited at 150 psig and 500°.

I walked around the pint-sized steam turbine, wondering what I had gotten myself into. ***I was now trapped in what seemed like a bad dream.*** The difference between this and a dream is that in a dream, you wake-up to reality. I was already in my reality. There was nothing good to wake up to.

I didn't know it then, but what the plant lacked in size was more than made up for in complexity. I had a vertical learning curve in front of me. This was my first plant that was entirely DCS-controlled. DCS stands for Distributed Control System. Simply put, the controls to run this unit were on interactive display screens only, without hardware-based switches, buttons, dials, gauges, meters, or alarm panels.

Turns out that this small, coal-fired, fluidized-bed boiler was crazy-complex. In the 1980s, fluidized bed units were considered the answer to burning coal cleanly. Unfortunately, they were extremely high maintenance and problematic to keep operating.

The control room of this tiny plant was on the second floor next to the turbine room. It was a long, narrow room that seemed almost like an afterthought. It was one of the few areas of the plant that had activity in it. A young, heavy-set, round-faced man with a short, gnarly beard walked swiftly over to me.

"Are you from Burns and McDonnell Engineering?" He spoke rapidly, and immediately appeared to be very high-strung.

"Mark Gregg." I stretched my right hand out. He shook it vigorously. His radio was attached to his hip, but the large, square microphone was clipped to his lapel with a coiled cable hanging loosely down to the radio. He reminded me of a dog that broke his leash.

He reached up and keyed the mic, twisting his head like a dog trying to scratch a flea on its neck, "Kevin, come to the control room." He then turned his head back and locked eyes with me. "I'm Rick Crown, the Plant Superintendent." He sized me up for a moment. "So, you are the new operational expert from Burns and McDonnell?"

I smiled. "Is that how they billed me?"

"Damn sure better be based on what they are charging us!"

I was taken aback by this. He seemed serious, but I wasn't sure. As it turns out, *he was.* When dealing with AGM personnel, money was the name of the game... Okay, money was the *only* game. The Managers at the AGM *never* joked about money. It was an obsession.

The door on the back side of the control room opened, and an even younger man, slender and ruggedly handsome, walked up to me. Rick turned to him.

"Kevin, this is Mark Craig from Burns and McDonnell. He is our new operational expert."

I reached out to shake Kevin's hand. "My name is Mark Gregg, not Craig. *I have two first names.*"

Kevin shook my hand and said, "Craig and Gregg are both first names." He then smiled broadly. He seemed far less intense than Rick. He also had a look of intelligence about him as he grinned and said, "My name is Kevin Nordlowe. I have two first names also." He then grimaced slightly. "I am the Assistant Plant Superintendent."

"Pleased to meet you both." I smiled loosely but wasn't even slightly relaxed.

Rick jumped right into things with no chit-chat. After all, chit-chat is time, and time is money.

"We are doing the final DCS loop-checks while ASEA is making some modifications to the boiler bed transfer system." He looked at me condescendingly. "How much fluidized bed boiler experience do you bring to the table?"

To say the least, I was blown away by his inquiry. He obviously didn't see or look at my resume. I forced another lame smile, looked at my watch, and said, "Looks like about 12 minutes, as of right now."

They both gave me a courtesy laugh. Rick then looked at me skeptically. "You gotta have steel-toed shoes, safety glasses with side shields, and an approved hard hat to be in the plant." I was wearing my steel toed shoes and hard hat from Bonanza (my previous plant) but didn't have safety glasses. He looked at Kevin as he turned to walk away. "Kevin, take him to the plant storehouse and get him ready to work."

Kevin and I walked to the warehouse. They referred to it as the plant storehouse or sometimes just "stores." I was surprised at how young both Rick and Kevin were. Kevin explained that they were the only two management people in the cogen plant. Both He and Rick were mechanical engineers. He was fresh out of school, and Rick had only been out for a couple of years.

AGM would select a good engineering school and hire from the top 20% of the class, bringing them in as managers. Not manager trainees but *full* managers right out of the proverbial box. AGM wanted people who were moldable and did not have *any* habits, let alone bad ones. It reminded me of Proverbs 22:6…

"Train up a child in the way he should go and when he is old, he will not depart from it."

AGM wanted managers who were dyed-in-the-wool AGM thinkers. There was no room for dissent or non-compliance in any form. They were the largest grain millers in the world and, therefore *must* be doing everything correctly.

I cannot say enough about how flawed this logic could be. Bringing in a boy raised on the farm with real-life experience and an engineering degree could work and even work well, depending on the individual. However, bringing in a kid with no significant life experience or previous work skills who ONLY had an engineering degree could be a disaster in the making. I saw it go both ways at AGM (and other places) later in my career.

After getting my safety glasses with Kevin, he told me to get some prints and walk the plant down so I could be useful to them. I thought Burns and McDonnell engineered this plant, but they were only responsible for the high-pressure piping and the electrical. Everything else was "field erected".

This simply means there was not necessarily proper engineering completed before construction, and the builders worked largely from verbal directions, primarily from Rick Crown, and not prints.

I was exhausted that first evening. I grabbed a burger from McDonalds and then called Vangie and the kids from my hotel room. I was already missing them badly, and it was only my first day. Vangie was cold and distant. She assured me that she was getting the house settled *despite my absence.*

She found out which school Brandi and Brittanie should attend from the next-door neighbors. It was Park Avenue Elementary. She enrolled them that afternoon. She said it was an older school, but the girl's teachers appeared to be nice. They would be walking about a block to catch the school bus each day. I then talked to the kids. Brittanie was excited about school. She was almost 8 years old. Brandi was almost 11 years old and was not even slightly enthused about the new school, Des Moines, or the move in general. I certainly couldn't blame her.

Brandi struggled with all our moves far more than Brittanie or Josh did. I also started realizing just how difficult this was on Vangie. She was forced to handle **EVERYTHING** associated with coming to a new town, PLUS taking care of three kids and a small dog. Looking back on it, I did not see just how big of an idiot I was and how much stress was thrown on her. She was an angel and deserved far better.

The first week in Mankato went quickly. I jumped right in and worked with them, doing loop checks as well as hustling to figure out this beast of a plant. They had not fired the boiler yet but had loaded sand in the lower bed and began using the pneumatic bed elevators to move it up and down. The pneumatic bed elevator system was complex, and there was substantially more complexity associated with other systems on this crazy boiler.

With each passing day, the plant became more challenging. AGM's plan was to run this plant with one person on back-shifts and only four people during weekday day shifts, including him and Rick. AGM certainly didn't believe in bloated staff structures.

One person on the back-shifts and weekends? That person must run the plant, keep coal in the silo, handle ash removal, check water chemistry, and deal with any other issues that arose.

This seemed impossible and even dangerous to me. There were a ton of stairs and ladders in the plant to reach valves and equipment. In addition to all this, the original package boiler that supplied process steam to the grain plant was moved to the cogen plant as the steam backup. A single

11

back-shift operator also had to take care of that boiler. Tall order. A tall order indeed. *Now for the real kicker...*

My entire time with AGM convinced me they viewed the cogeneration plant as a low-priority *nuisance* to the central purpose of grain milling. Prior to the cogen plant, they spent years operating small, gas-fired package boilers that ran primarily unattended while purchasing needed electrical power from the local utilities. It couldn't get any easier than this.

With the advent of the cogen plant, they were now generating their own power using an extremely complex, high-pressure, fluidized bed boiler supplying a steam turbine that served as a steam pressure and temperature-reducing station. That reducing station supplied the process plant with steam at the proper pressure and temperature while providing the required electrical power for the plant. Nothing could be simpler, *right?*

Now, for the ultimate proof that power generation existed in another, lesser realm at AGM... When it came time to provide staff for the cogeneration facility, the corn and soybean plant managers sent what appeared to be their *rejects* to Rick and Kevin. Rick and Kevin did not hire their people from any kind of qualified pool.

The corn and soybean plant Managers hired people they considered suitable for this kind of work, and it appeared they sent the inferior, unteachable, and problematic personnel to the cogen. Even worse, the people hired in the corn and soybean plant appeared to be hired for one of two reasons... Nepotism, or friendship. Aptitude didn't appear to be part of the hiring process.

The exception to this was the Managers. As stated, they would hire the best of the best from the engineering programs at a couple of top universities. These people were tasked with getting the job done with the tools they were given. *Believe me, some of the people they were given were real tools.*

Abraham Maslow, an American Psychologist, was credited with the statement, ***"To a man with a hammer, everything looks like a nail."*** Due to my insecurity working around two top-notch engineers (or at least one and a half... The jury was still out on Rick), I knew I had to fill a gap somewhere. It only took a few days to realize that the four operators who moved from the grain plant to the cogen plant were, at best, problematic. However, *they became my nails!* I immediately started working with them to instill some level of competence to run this very complex plant.

While they all had learning issues, the scariest one was Bob Randolf. He was in his late 50's but looked much older. He was so large that the only thing he could wear was bibb overalls... Bibb overalls that were always *filthy.* Apparently, he experienced a stroke a few years earlier and could no longer manage (nor hold) his bowels and bladder. Anyway, this was the excuse he used. I think he was just a slob.

Bob wore heavy spectacles, the left lens being much thicker than the right lens. This magnified his left eye to be much larger than the other. When you looked at him, it was akin to looking at a Cyclops because you would instinctively focus only on his huge left eye. His voice shook with an induced staccato that directly matched the frequency of his quaking hands. Honestly, this man should have been in an assisted care facility. Unfortunately, it gets worse, much, *much* worse.

Bob had a girlfriend. She was far less than half his age, very obese, and mentally challenged. She had at least three children and was in a continuous state of lactation. She would bring him lunch or dinner at the plant, and she never wore a bra; she usually just wore a T-shirt. Rick nicknamed her *"slippery-tit"*. Yes, crude, unfeeling, insensitive, and mean. Unfortunately, it fit the situation.

Her youngest child was always hanging from one arm, usually in a crapped-up diaper. When he fussed, she would simply plop down wherever she was, lift her T-shirt, and feed him. Her hair was never combed, her face was rarely clean, and the children were even less kept than her. It was a sad sight, and I felt terribly bad for her kids every time I saw them. I just didn't know what to do for them.

Bob's lack of control over his waste elimination processes relegated him to one special chair in the control room. It was not special in its design, it was special because of the putrescent, gag-inducing odor. NO ONE would get near Bob's 'special' chair. If you accidentally sat on it, you would excuse yourself and find some place to change your britches, ridding yourself of the foul odor that would accompany you wherever you went.

It was common to see Rick, Kevin, or one of the operators wheel the chair out to the boiler room to let it air out. Rick would occasionally ask the contract maintenance people to carry it to the basement and hose it off, letting it dry in a warm area by the boiler. My experiences with Bob remained with me for a lifetime, and not just because of his personal hygiene as we will cover later.

I worked extensively with the operators to help them learn the fundamentals of plant operation and, specifically

14

how to operate *this* plant. This was the very first (of three) boilers like this that ASEA ever built. AGM owned all three of them. Unfortunately, this boiler was not working even close to its design parameters.

During our continuous attempts to make this boiler operate properly on coal we were filling the ash silo with our coal/ash waste. This massive ash silo had two pug-mills that were designed to convey the ash from the silo into a waiting trailer below. The pug mills introduced spray water to keep the ash as dustless as possible while conveying it into the semi-trucks parked under the discharge chute. The AGM plant was on the outskirts of Mankato, and excessive dust in or near the town would have been intolerable.

I accompanied Kevin to the silo as we observed the operator placing the pug-mill in service. The spent ash/limestone mixture from the fluidized bed boiler was readily flowing through the pug-mill and filled the large, 18 - wheel, semi-truck parked under the silo. We quickly, almost effortlessly, finished loading the first truck, and he moved forward to allow the second truck access to the dump area under the silo.

About 45 seconds after he moved the truck out from under the silo, there was a seismic, visceral, gut-wrenching **_WHOOOOM_** akin to a rocket being launched. In a split second, the *ENTIRE* contents of the semi-trailer blew at least 200 feet straight into the sky, leaving the trailer empty and *completely* clean. The mammoth, dense ash cloud was primarily dark gray with a tinge of red in it and eventually left a visible layer of dust over the entire northeast side of Mankato. The sides of the trailer were extremely hot and had it not blown straight into the air, anyone it contacted would have been severely, if not mortally, burned.

15

Kevin and I locked eyes for several moments in stunned, terrified disbelief. After the initial shock, Kevin looked at me with crazy eyes and screamed, *"WHAT THE HELL JUST HAPPENED?"*

I lifted my arms and shrugged my shoulders, shaking my head in astonishment. It was obviously an exothermic reaction caused by mixing water with the spent ash/limestone in the silo. The crazy thing about it was the time delay. It took about three to five minutes to fill the truck and then another 45 or so seconds after the driver pulled out of the unloading area before it disgorged into the atmosphere. We dodged a *huge* bullet on this one.

From that point forward, it became a major production to unload the ash silo and keep the ash in the trucks. We could not use any water to mute the light ash due to the chemical reaction causing extreme heat.

We eventually had to unload the ash, dry, into the trucks very slowly and then immediately tarp the trailers to prevent the dry, dusty ash from blowing everywhere. What was supposed to be a minor, quick operation became a 45-minute, per truck pain in the butt. Yet, AGM still planned to run this plant with one operator on the backshift and weekends.

Yes, the learning curve at this plant was vertical for everyone, including me. As we moved forward with keeping the plant running, it became increasingly difficult. I found myself at the plant anytime Bob Randolf was there. He was incapable of making informed operating decisions of any sort, requiring Rick to manipulate the operator's schedule to double-team him. The other operators would be held over or brought in early, but due to such a small staff, *I was being forced to babysit him and run the plant when they weren't available.*

I was doing my very best to teach Bob and the others, but the parameters of operation continuously changed due to issues with the boiler. It required having your wits about you continuously while constantly thinking about the overall process. Unfortunately, Bob had a problem with thinking. The other operators were poor, at best, but were lightyears ahead of Bob in their understanding of the plant.

Originally, I was supposed to be in Mankato for a month or so, but the construction progress at the Des Moines plant wasn't moving as fast as planned, leaving me unneeded there. Plus, due to the problems at this plant, I was forced to remain in Mankato and drive home most weekends. I was beginning to detest being a babysitter to Bob but thoroughly enjoyed operating this complex little conundrum of a power plant.

Not unlike when I was forced to be at the Craig Plant training the Intermountain operators, I began struggling with depression. It was made much worse by sensing that Vangie and I were getting more distant. She was miserable, and I was miserable. Mostly for the same reasons. She was forced to be a single mother, with me having little or no influence or interactions with the kids.

The ONLY positive thing about this entire situation was the amount of money I was earning. There was no overtime, but I was paid straight time for every hour worked. I worked ridiculously long hours every day I was there. Plus, the tax-free per diem and housing stipend added up very quickly.

17

Fall sequenced to winter. If you have never experienced winter in Minnesota, you are lucky. Many years after my Minnesota winter, I spent several weeks at Prudhoe Bay in Alaska. It is in the Arctic Circle and close to the North Pole. I was there in the dead of winter, where the daily temperature was about -45° F every single day. However, Mankato seemed colder. It felt like the wind blew continuously, and the humidity in Mankato was always high. You were continuously hot in the summer and inconsolably cold in the winter.

The drive to and from Mankato was treacherous on more than one occasion as I made the round-trip no matter how bad the weather. The little Hyundai became an ice-ball on more than one trek to and from Des Moines to Mankato. My only solace in this self-made hell was coming home to be with Vangie and the kids. Unfortunately, the only thing colder than the Mankato winter was Vangie. She bore the brunt of my ego issues in Vernal and my consistently poor decisions that led us to Des Moines.

Vangie sometimes tells a story to others about how she was coping without me. The worst and most often repeated one is when I came home on a Friday night and stepped quietly into the house, showering and climbing into bed with her. She awakened long enough to verify it was me and then rolled over and went back to sleep.

The next morning, she and the kids awakened, ate breakfast, and piled into the Wagoneer to go to the shopping mall to walk, play, and shop. She backed out of the driveway and onto the street before *remembering I was even home.* She slowly pulled back into the driveway and opened the garage door only to see me standing there looking wholly crushed, dejected, and saddened by our disconnect. She still likes telling this story. Unfortunately, it was an entirely true story. *I still hate hearing it.*

As we slid helplessly into the cold winter months, my involvement at the Mankato plant began taking a troubling turn. Looking back, I realize it was the logical progression under the circumstances, but certainly not what I had envisioned when I took this job. Another train wreck was about to happen, I just didn't see it coming at that moment.

CHAPTER 3

BOB RANDOLF AND THE COFFEE POT

January 1988 was extremely cold in Mankato. A fresh snow turned the Minnesota prairie frigid, with the humidity and wind working viciously, depriving those who endured of any comfort whatsoever. It wasn't just cold, it was **bitter, bone-numbing cold.**

As usual, we were struggling to keep the plant running. It was Monday morning, and I drove the four-hour drive from Des Moines to Mankato, arriving at the plant about 8:00 a.m. Normally, we started work at or before 7:00 a.m., but Rick tried to cut me some slack on Monday mornings and Friday afternoons due to my travel to and from Des Moines.

Unfortunately, that Monday we encountered numerous, taxing issues while keeping the plant operating. Rick and Kevin were tense, and I was tired and barely tolerating Rick's bad mood. Even worse, Bob Randolf was scheduled to work that afternoon.

It was crucial in this cold environment to keep the plant operating to provide steam to the corn and soybean plant for revenue, but also *to keep everything from freezing.* If the fluidized bed unit and steam turbine went down, it was essential to get the gas-fired package boiler running ASAP to ensure heat in the entire facility.

At about 5:00 p.m., Rick pulled me aside. I was worn-out and ready to drop.

"Mark, you need to stay as late as possible and help Bob keep this plant running. We can't afford to lose revenue in the grain plant, or worse, freezing everything."

I had carte blanche to spend as much time as I wanted at the plant and normally tried to give him every hour he asked for. I made $45,000.00 in taxable income in 1988. This, along with the tax-free per diem and housing stipend, was a decent amount of money for the time. The problem was, I was physically and mentally exhausted that afternoon. Unfortunately, I had no choice but to bite the bullet and help Bob.

Once everyone was gone except for myself and Bob, I was able to 'dial-in' and fine-tune the plant so that it was running like a Swiss watch. It is amazing how attuned and aware you can become of a plant process such as this one.

I could be anywhere in the plant amidst the cacophony of mechanical pandemonium and yet still clearly hear and feel individual, barely perceptible noises, vibrations, and sounds that were even slightly abnormal. It was a sixth sense of sorts. I have worked around operators all my life, and most seem to develop this sixth sense over time. It is not unlike a mother being attune to the noises her child makes. The slightest variation reaches out and grabs their attention.

I became uncomfortably cold as I hadn't eaten since I arrived at the plant and had been running hard all day long. At about 9:30 p.m., Bob was asleep in his chair, and I was nodding off and *extremely* hungry. I knew if I didn't leave soon, I wouldn't find any fast-food places open.

Because the plant was running well, I decided it would be okay to leave Bob in front of the consoles... I would grab a bite to eat and get a little sleep, returning later. Even more than filling my belly with food, I was looking forward to a hot shower and getting some of the chill out of my bones. I was inconsolably cold.

"Bob, Bob, wake up." I nudged his shoulder. Wow! This guy really stunk tonight. I nudged him a second time. "Wake up, Bob."

He snarfled and awakened with a start. "What's wwwrong... Is something wrong?"

"Nothing is wrong, Bob." I raised my voice because poor old Bob was about deaf. "I am going to the motel to get a little rest." I grabbed a pen and piece of paper and wrote the motel phone number and my room number on it. "If *ANYTHING* happens, or if you need something, call this number and I will come back and help you."

Bob held the piece of paper up to whichever eye was good, it seemed to change based on conditions. "Oookaaayyy... Are you sure you must leeeaavvee?" His voice was always grating but combined with the involuntary quaking, it was quite aggravating. I mean, I truly felt bad for him, but he would get under your skin very quickly.

"Bob, it will be fine. You shouldn't have to do anything except keep an eye on the console. Let me know if something goes wrong." I made one last check of the major parameters on the console. The plant looked good and seemed to be running very well. I then slipped out of the warmth of the plant into the windy, icy, frozen hell. I finally learned what people meant by the statement, "When hell freezes over!" It's a real thing. *It is Mankato, Minnesota in the winter.*

McDonalds was about to close, but I was able to get a burger and fries... The staple of life when you are on the road. I woofed them down in large, partially chewed gulps. As I drove recklessly to the motel, I threw the empty McDonalds bag into the back seat with several others that were taking permanent residence there.

Finally, a hot shower. I soaked in the heavenly drizzle until my body slowly transitioned to a bright pink and, for the first time in several hours, felt warm. The combination of a full belly and the warm shower completely relaxed me and total exhaustion took over.

I set the alarm for 5:00 a.m. and wrapped up in the blankets. The clock said 11:07. I am relatively certain I was fast asleep seconds after my head hit the pillow.

BEEBEEBEEBEEBEEP.

BEEBEEBEEBEEBEEP.

My whole body spasmed, startled by the funky ringer on the motel phone right next to my head. I partially sat up, grabbed the handset, and thrust it to my ear. "Hello!" I was trying to focus. I noticed the clock said 11:41. I had slept about 30 minutes.

"*Maaarrrk, this is BBBob.*" He drew a labored breath. "*Thiiiinggs are reeeaaall baaaad here.*" That was it. That's all he said and then he hung up the phone. *Who does that?*

I tried calling him back, but he never answered. I jumped-up and threw on my clothes, and stepped into the inhospitable deep freeze called Minnesota. There was virtually no traffic, so I was back at the plant within 10 minutes.

I kept my eyes peeled for flames, excessive vapor, emergency vehicles, or anything else that would indicate a disaster at the plant during the drive there. However, there was nothing other than the stack had no water vapor coming out of it. I knew this meant trouble.

The very moment I entered the front door I knew something was amiss. Everything sounded out of kilter. The fans were running, but oddly muffled. My first thought was that the bed must be slumped and the fans weren't moving any air.

I could hear the turbine bypass valve squealing as it supplied steam to the process plant due to the turbine being tripped. I also picked-up on an odd whine and a vibration that shouldn't have been there. There was no question the plant was sorely screwed-up.

Entering the control room, two things stood out. Bob was nowhere to be found, and hundreds of alarms were ringing on the console. Sure enough, the bed was slumped and was only about 900°. If it were above 1050°, I could reintroduce coal, but at 900°, I must use the gas burners. The fans were at minimum, explaining their muffled sound out in the plant. There were three more items that seriously alarmed me.

The first issue was the steam-driven bed-circulation pump. Because there are steam generation tubes located within the fluidized bed, you must ALWAYS keep water circulating through them and back to the drum when the unit is hot. In a loss of power, a steam-driven backup would automatically start to ensure the tubes did not melt. *This backup pump was running.*

The second, far more concerning issue, was the steam turbine was spinning at about half speed and did not appear to be tripped. Technically, this was way wrong. The generator was offline. The vibration on the steam turbine was far above the trip point. Most of the steam turbine indications on the console were displaying gut-wrenching ##### symbols. I had no way of telling what was happening on the steam turbine. I was essentially blind due to the DCS not displaying data.

Without it, you are clueless about what was happening in the plant.

The third was the drum level, which was out the top of the drum. Who knows how much water was being pushed into the steam lines? This scared me more than anything. A water hammer on a steam system like this can rip the piping off the hangars and possibly even rip open a steam line. Fortunately, there were no water hammers at that moment.

I punched the manual trip override buttons for the steam turbine and the boiler feed pumps. I heard the turbine's main steam stop valve clunk as it slammed closed. When a plant is operated entirely by DCS (using computer displays and not hardware), they are required to have manual trip override buttons on major equipment in the event the DCS software or hardware fails. This was the first time I had to use these buttons, other than testing them early in the commissioning phase of the plant.

I then began commanding many of the steam drains open to rid the steam lines of condensate. Unfortunately, the DCS was not responding. This was starting to make sense. Something in the DCS had glitched or locked, partially explaining why things were so wonky.

I hesitantly initiated a reboot of the DCS system. This was a HUGE issue and should never be necessary because all the control systems would shut down and then restart. There was now nothing I could do in the control room while the DCS system was doing a reboot.

The steam pressure was now down to about 300 psi, and the soybean plant was about to lose steam. This was the worst-case scenario. I ran as hard and fast as I could down the stairs and to the gas-fired auxiliary boiler. It had a steam heating coil in the lower drum that kept it partially warm, so a quick start could be done. I hoped Bob was there starting it. Again, he was nowhere to be found.

I initiated a start sequence on the auxiliary boiler and waited out the purge. As soon as it finished purging and lit off, I went to manual with the pressure controller and fired it ridiculously hard to get the pressure in the main header to start increasing again.

Firing the auxiliary boiler this hard produced a deep, bone jarring rumble that resonated throughout the plant. I found it exhilarating even though it was potentially damaging the boiler to fire this aggressively.

When the steam header pressure finally began increasing, I placed the pressure controller back in AUTO and sprinted back to the control room.

I finished doing some necessary procedures for the restart of the DCS. It now appeared to be working properly. The steam turbine data was displaying correctly, and I was able to open the steam drains and prepare for a proper restart. I had no idea how much damage, if any, was done to the turbine but I was determined to get this plant back up.

The restart had many issues, forcing me to work painstakingly through each one of them. It was about 4:30 in the morning when Bob finally lumbered back into the control room. The fluidized bed boiler was again firing coal, and the steam turbine/generator was now connected to the electrical system, with the steam turbine supplying the steam header as it was supposed to. The only thing I had not yet completed was bringing the auxiliary boiler back to standby operation. It was idling but still firing.

"Where in the hell have you been?" I angrily asked Bob as he sheepishly slogged over to his chair.

Bob looked at me mournfully and then slowly said, "Things gggot really baaaad and I went to the soybean pppplant to get a cup of cccoffee."

That was his entire explanation. He offered no other reason as to why he would randomly leave the control room.

"What do you think caused the plant to go down like it did?" I was so angry I wanted seriously to punch him in the throat. However, I needed to figure out what happened before Rick and Kevin arrived.

He slowly shook his head and painfully trudged over to the coffee pot. "The coffee pppot quit wwworking, and I knew I had to stay awake with you being gggone. I think the circuit bbbreaker for the coffee pppot tripped."

I could not believe the conversation went from nearly destroying the plant to a non-working coffee pot. "Did you check the breaker on the electrical outlet that the coffee pot is plugged into?" I asked disgustedly.

"I didn't know wwwhere it was, so I rrrreset a whole bbbbunch of them in the backroom."

This sent me reeling. *I knew then what happened*. "Bob, how did you reset a bunch of them?"

"You know wwwhat I am ttttalking about... You ccclick them off, and then bbbback on... This is how you rrreset those small bbbreakers."

"Show me the panel or panels you switched them off and then back on." I was trying as hard as possible to not show my intense, burning rage. I was honestly fighting the urge to scream at him, telling him how stupid he was.

We walked slowly into the *control logic room* that he innocently called, "the backroom". This was the most critical area in the entire plant. The electronic equipment for the control systems as well as a multitude of vital small circuit breakers were located there for all the critical control circuits.

Most of them received power from the plant battery bank that supplied power to them through a D.C. to A.C. inverter. These were the circuit breakers that powered transmitters, control loops, and the plant logic systems.

There was nothing more critical in the plant than these circuit breakers, and Bob randomly flipped them off and back on trying to get the damn coffee pot working!

I was filled with rage and wanted to truly hurt Bob. However, I explained to him as coolly as I could that he should NEVER come into this room again *under any circumstances* and certainly should never randomly open and close circuit breakers without knowing what they fed. He seemed ambivalent about the entire discussion.

I went into the restroom, locked the door, and began repeating a prayer that was becoming more routine in recent weeks. "Lord, I can't continue with this. It has been over five months, and I miss Vangie and the kids. I am getting nowhere, and I don't think I can keep doing this. I know I messed-up in Vernal, but I need YOUR help now. *I can't keep doing this.*"

Rick and Kevin arrived around 7:00 that morning. I was so insanely tired I was feeling punchy. The plant was still running, and Bob was getting relieved by the dayshift operator. I walked into Rick's office and told him and Kevin exactly what happened that night, right down to the coffee pot fiasco.

28

When I finished gushing about my trainwreck of a night, Rick looked at me morosely and said, "I guess you need to do a helluva lot better job training Bob."

I completely lost my sanity for a moment and I lashed out angrily. "The man isn't trainable!" I raised my voice even louder. "He is dumber than a brick and a danger to himself and everyone else! He should not be working here!" I could feel my jaw jutting and my face turning hot. "I could train a monkey to run this plant easier than I could train Bob!"

Kevin wryly interjected, "Makes sense to me. A monkey is smarter and has a much greater attention span…"

It was at that moment I knew I was done. I looked at them and said, "Guys, I am going to the motel to get some rest." The resignation in my voice was evident.

Arriving back at the motel, I called Steve Swain and told him I would quit unless Burns and McDonnell moved me to the Des Moines cogen. I told him what I was up against and I would not do it any longer. Steve was apologetic and told me not to do anything until he talked to other Burns personnel and got back to me.

The phone next to my bed awakened me from a deep sleep at about 2:00 p.m. It was Steve Swain.

"Mark, I talked to the Project Manager for the AGM contract. He talked to the AGM folks about Des Moines and Mankato. He wants you to give them three more weeks at Mankato, and then you can start in Des Moines on Monday, March 7th. The plant is still not quite ready, but they felt they could probably use you in Des Moines, then."

We talked for a bit longer. I decided to finish this week in Mankato and take a few days off, staying in Des Moines

Saturday through Tuesday and coming back to Mankato on Wednesday. It was a good decision. The four days at home were badly needed.

I reluctantly gave them three more weeks in Mankato. It was difficult, and I have never been back there since leaving after that third week. Obviously, it would not bother me if I never saw Mankato again.

The one issue I failed to consider about going to the Des Moines plant was losing the per-diem and my carte blanche to work as many hours as I wanted. There would be no per-diem in Des Moines because it was considered my home base. While the extended hours eventually happened in Des Moines, it was a few months out and even then, it was just for a short period of time. It didn't matter. Money was becoming *far* less important in the face of a disintegrating family life.

CHAPTER 4
LINCOLN, NEBRASKA

My first day at the Des Moines Cogen introduced me to Jerry Rime. He was the Plant Superintendent. He was young and considerably overweight. He had blonde, curly locks framing his plump, perpetually red face and appeared to be quite intelligent, a fact that was proven over the course of our time working together.

Jerry's personality was the diametrical opposite of Rick Crown in Mankato. Rick was excitable and intense. Jerry was about as laid back and cerebral as possible. Rick would run where angels feared to tread, whereas Jerry would simply ruminate, make observations, and then send someone to do his bidding. He was a good manager, especially considering his young age.

Unlike Mankato, Des Moines had two assistant managers, and neither were engineers. The first was Tom Hickman. He was in his mid to late 30's and a nice guy. He wasn't the sharpest knife in the drawer, but was easy to get along with. If you had even a slightly good argument, he would believe anything you told him. I think the word for this is *gullible*.

One day, I told Tom that electricity was much more efficient when going forward than when going backward. He astutely grunted and said, "I knew that was the case from my previous studies." He was dead serious. He didn't even know I was joking. I felt so bad that I never corrected my statement.

The other assistant to Jerry was an old, gray, and bitter curmudgeon named Bud Lindley. He was eternally moody and difficult to read. His only concern in the plant was the coal handling system. It seemed this was all he was suited for anyway. He and I never talked much. He mostly had a permanent scowl on his face except for quitting time each day. I did my best to let him do his coal-handling duties and stayed out of his way.

I was also introduced to another AGM employee named John Starnes. John was in his early 20s, brilliant, immature, and usually one step ahead of everyone. He was their lead engineer for the DCS systems.

This young man was about as sarcastic as anyone I have ever known, even to this day. As I write this memoir, I became aware that John is still with AGM in a lofty management position. This is AGM's way. Hire a brilliant mind fresh out of school and keep them forever. John was a good choice. For as young and immature as he was, he understood logic and process control *incredibly* well.

At Des Moines, I was the go-to guy along with John Starnes. John was immersed in the DCS system and knew every logic statement and control algorithm in the plant. His intelligence helped him turn this to a real understanding of the plant and not just theoretical. However, I was the only person in Des Moines who spent countless hours running the Mankato facility and dealing with the operational issues. I was truly the experienced, operational professional here.

I went from training operators and keeping a low profile at Mankato to being appreciated for my experience and knowledge of the Des Moines plant. It was a nice change, but I didn't let it go to my head. I was keenly aware that Jerry and John were incredibly smart, and I had to be as accurate as possible in everything I did to stay ahead or remain even with them.

Jerry, Tom, Bud, and I started going to lunch on a frequent basis. John rarely accompanied us because he was continuously going Mach-3 with his hair on fire. The DCS was a critical path on the start-up and still needed a ton of work.

We would frequently bring John something back from lunch, and he would annihilate it in a matter of seconds and then get back to his work without even wiping his hands or face. Watching him eat was like watching a dog dive voraciously into a bowl of warm beef gravy. John could lick the bowl clean without missing a stroke on his keypad.

It took a couple of weeks at home in Des Moines before life started becoming more normal for us. The kids started understanding that Daddy was back home and not just visiting. Vangie and I's relationship was slowly thawing. However, I could tell there was serious damage done to our bond, but it did seem to be slowly healing.

Initially, I was working normal office hours at the Des Moines plant. This allowed us to do things with the kids as a family, including shopping, walking in the mall, and even sledding on a hill that was near our house. Later, as the weather warmed, we were able to use the boat again at Saylorville Reservoir right outside of the Des Moines metro area.

We visited the Iowa State capitol building and a few museums as we became a family again. It was truly appreciated. Vangie deserved a husband, and the kids deserved a dad. Up till now, we had been a fractured family due to my time in Mankato.

We also started attending Church again. We found an Assembly of God Church on Army Post Road. It was nice to attend Church again, and important for us to get the kids back into suitable Children's ministries. *When we were finally all together, life in Des Moines seemed almost normal.* I realized just how much we lost when I ran from Vernal. *It was a life-long lesson that I would never forget.*

It was around this time I started hearing about Brad Johnson at the AGM Lincoln cogen. Rick and Kevin had thrown shade at him when I was in Mankato. I knew I would be relegated to Lincoln when the Des Moines plant was running, and I was dreading being gone again like I was with the Mankato plant. Plus, Brad's reputation was far-reaching. He was the Plant Superintendent at Lincoln and was headstrong, brash, hard to work with, and apparently very outspoken about *everything.*

During this time at the Des Moines cogen plant, I began building personal computers in the evenings after the kids went to bed. In 1988, there was still a ton of mystery and bewilderment concerning personal computers. Building one was simply a matter of buying a 1" thick (or more) catalog called *"Computer Shopper."* You could browse seemingly endless ads for off-brand personal computers and every conceivable personal computer part imaginable. Most of the parts and pieces were from China or Taiwan, but they were cheap, generic, and generally worked well.

After buying the basic parts, such as a case, power supply, motherboard, CPU, keyboard, hard disk drive, etc. etc., you could assemble the computer relatively quickly. If you chose the parts well, you would usually have a decent product. Not always, but usually. The only real technical part of the assembly was installing the Microsoft DOS operating system on the hard disk drive.

I took the first computer I ever built to the Des Moines plant and set it up in my makeshift office. Just like at Engineering Physics (EP), I started using it for memos, procedures, graphics, etc. Because command-based DOS was the only operating system in those days I always built a simple menu system that allowed new users to easily start and use a simple graphics program and 'shareware' word processor.

Most people wanted to enter the personal computer age but were pensive about finding a "jumping-off" point to get started. The DOS operating system in those early days of PC's was 'command-based', requiring the user to remember the syntax. This scared most people away from computers at the time. By building the simple menu system, I would unintentionally draw people in as they saw how easy it was to use compared to just using the DOS command line.

Without really trying to sell these computers, word got out in the plant that they could buy a good computer relatively inexpensively. I don't know who spread this through the plant. Okay, *maybe it was me.* I enjoyed building them, and while not getting rich by any means, I put some extra cash in the bank doing it. Computer sales supplemented our income from losing the massive overtime I was getting in Mankato.

Overall, the plant start-up went smoothly in Des Moines. The operators that eventually migrated to the plant were substantially better than the Mankato operators. I enjoyed working with everyone at Des Moines, and they seemed to like me.

Unfortunately, Des Moines was short-lived. We only had the plant running for a couple of weeks when Jerry asked me into his office. It was a Friday afternoon, and I was getting ready to leave for the day.

"Mark, I have some good news and bad news for you." He was masking a look of concern on his face with an obvious phony smile. "The budget won't carry your salary here in Des Moines any longer, so they want you to start at the Lincoln cogen immediately."

I was caught off-guard and was completely stunned. There was absolutely no forewarning of this. I tried to remain aloof.

"Which is the good news, and which is the bad news?" I asked pensively.

Jerry's eyes darted nervously around the room as he gave a strained laugh. "I guess it depends on your perspective." He paused for a moment and his voice took on a sincere air of concern. "Mark, try not to get crossways with Brad. He is the ultimate micro-manager, and everything must be his way or nothing."

"When is this effective?"

"Unfortunately, *today*." Jerry's face turned crimson from embarrassment as he continued. "You need to be at the cogen plant in Lincoln on Monday morning." He stood and held out his right hand. "You truly did a great job here, and I want you to know I appreciate it."

I looked him in the eye and shook his hand while trying not to show the absolute flood of emotion reeling out of control in my mind.

"Thanks, Jerry. I enjoyed working here. I wish it could have been a little longer, but at least they are ready for me in Lincoln, so I am not being laid-off."

As I turned to leave, Jerry remorsefully said, "Mark, I am sorry you had no notice of this. The decision came from way above my salary level."

I walked into the control room and said goodbye to the operators and then found Bud and Tom and said goodbye to them. I was in a complete and utter state of shock. I didn't see this coming. I wasn't sure if I did something wrong or what else may have caused it. I would never know. It was an AGM thing. They could be unpredictable. The Swedes working with the boiler used to commonly say in broken English, "AGM... A Great Mess."

Vangie was as shocked as I was by the sudden announcement that I was traveling again. She immediately went dark, asking no questions. I hated this. Added to the shock of Des Moines ending, I was struggling with every bad thing I had heard about Brad Johnson, the Plant Superintendent at Lincoln.

Monday morning came fast. I said goodbye to the kids Sunday night and then left for Lincoln at about 4:00 the next morning. The trip was an easy one. Unlike Mankato, it was interstate the entire way there. The plant was on the east side of Lincoln, and not far off the interstate, so I was able to get there in about two and a half hours.

Turned out that Brad was all they warned me about and more. Even though the Mankato, Des Moines, and Lincoln cogens were almost identical, Brad had inserted his hand into everything. Instead of using the same Swedish-built hammermill coal pulverizers used in the other two plants, Brad wouldn't accept them and purchased a single, variable-speed roller mill from Williams Patent Crusher and Pulverizer Company out of Pennsylvania.

If he had used the same hammermills as Mankato and Des Moines, he would have had spare parts and backup. His decision to use the Williams roller mill left him with one pulverizer and no back-up. Plus, he had to completely rework the design of the boiler fuel delivery system.

The Williams pulverizer required extra control parameters for temperature control and grinding element speed. These weren't needed on the hammermills at the other two plants. Therefore, Brad designed and implemented these loops himself.

His control design had a few flaws. During one of the first attempts to fire the boiler on coal, the mill caught fire destroying it and much of the surrounding equipment. *Que Sera, Sera... All it costs is money, right?*

The massive problems at Lincoln were staggering. I walked directly into a beehive and the bees were not friendly. It appeared Brad didn't even want me there. I think I was ordered there by someone far above Brad, probably as a last-ditch effort to help salvage his mess at the plant, and possibly his career.

During my entire three weeks, there was nothing but conflict, conflagration, and turmoil. I never had much of a chance to shine. Brad forced every person on the plant site, including me, to consult with him for every conceivable decision. He detested independent thought or actions and demanded blind loyalty to his, and only his decisions and direction. As stated, I did this for three weeks... It was two weeks longer than necessary. I made no impact whatsoever at this plant... Negative or positive.

I called Steve Swain and asked if there was any other work because I was not staying in Lincoln any longer. I explained the situation, expecting push-back. Instead, he seemed fully aware of the issues at Lincoln and told me that Burns and McDonnell had a much better, much longer-term project in Illinois.

A.E. Staley company had a new high-tech project at their massive grain processing facility in Decatur, Illinois. The plant consisted of two, 375,000 Lb/hr multi-solid fluidized bed boilers. The boilers were designed by the Battelle Laboratories in Columbus, OH.

These boilers were touted as the greatest thing since sliced bread. They would be coupled with an 80 MW steam turbine supplied by ABB out of Europe. The turbine was a partially condensing unit but used controllable, high-flow extractions. They were using the newest DCS in existence, the Foxboro I/A (Intelligent Automation) system.

In addition to all this, they conducted a grand, cutting-edge social experiment. It was billed as an exciting new way to work with union employees. Looking back on it, it was the most bizarre work situation I was ever involved with, and it was ultimately a *colossal* failure.

Staley was tired of incessant union issues and decided they were eliminating supervisors and managers, allowing the foxes to supervise the hen house. ***They decided to let the union personnel supervise themselves.*** They would handle their own schedules, sign and approve their own timesheets, and not be subject to anything but peer pressure from other union members. I spent almost a year observing the largest personnel workplace disaster to ever occur in modern America. News flash… ***It not only failed miserably, but it also failed on virtually every conceivable level.***

Unlike AGM, Staley paid Burns and McDonnell to engineer the *entire* plant, top to bottom. It was an extremely nice plant and very well engineered. I was proud to be part of it. Burns wanted me to oversee the entire plant start-up for them. They even flew me to Kansas City to meet with the Principal Engineers on the project to ensure I knew the importance of this project to Burns.

While I never heard the total amount, I know that Burns made millions on the project. This plant was very high profile within the power industry due to the leading-edge technology being used. Luckily, I was extremely careful not to allow my ego to override my senses as I did in Vernal.

At this point in time, I was totally clueless that I was about to experience an incredible, life-changing Divine intervention in the next several months. What was about to occur in the coming months was bizarre, and once again, God ordained and orchestrated and, again, *changed our lives forevever.*

CHAPTER 5
DECATUR, ILLINOIS

Our first major test was to find a place to live in Decatur. It was a medium-sized industrial town that had a massive AGM plant, the huge Staley plant that I was assigned to, as well as a host of other firms, including a company called Diesel Kiki. It was later renamed to Zexel. It was part of the Bosch conglomerate that was expanding to Decatur.

Diesel Kiki was importing dozens of people to manage their new facility. This made finding a place to live almost impossible due to the high demand.

During the first day of my first week there, I checked in at the Staley Plant and met Dave Hanson. Dave was the superintendent of the new cogeneration facility and a human resource person. It took very little conversation to realize he was not an engineer or technical person. He was squat, maybe 5'2", heavy, sloppily dressed, and ALWAYS had a dumb smile on his pock-marked face, having had deep pits from what was probably teenage acne. It was very hard not to like Dave Hanson. He was as easy-going as any person you could ever find.

Staley picked him to oversee the social experiment, allowing the union personnel to supervise themselves. In my opinion, Dave could have easily been replaced with a paper clip. He was a consummate people-pleaser. Again, he was an extremely likable, nice guy. It took his personality to oversee the trainwreck that occurred with Staley's approach to easing union issues.

Dave seemed genuinely pleased that I was "on-board" at the plant and told me to take "all the time I needed" to find a place to live. I think he was pleased there was someone with technical instincts to better buffer him from the union personnel. Then again, his personality would warmly welcome a known serial killer with open arms. Dave was the nicest, but poorest manager I ever worked with. I am still not sure if calling him a manager is even an appropriate term.

The drive to Decatur from our home in Des Moines was almost six hours. It took a full day there or a full day back to Des Moines. I knew I had to find a place to live as quickly as possible, but every avenue I took to find something decent was shut down, usually by someone from Diesel Kiki renting it first. As with Pavlov's salivating dogs, just the mention of Diesel Kiki sent shock waves down my spine.

I looked steadily that first week and found nothing even remotely viable to move Vangie and the kids into. I drove the long drive back to Des Moines, defeated and depressed. I knew I had to start working or go broke. Therefore, after a quick weekend in Des Moines, I was back to work Monday morning at the Staley Plant. Due to the six-hour drive, I had to leave late Sunday afternoon and spend the night in a motel in Decatur Sunday night. This required me to look for homes in the evenings or slip out during the day and lose pay. This went on for two more weeks.

The third weekend, I drove back to Des Moines with no news of a place to live. Vangie and I had a bad argument about our life (or lack thereof) to this point. I didn't blame her for being upset. It absolutely sucked driving back Friday night, getting in after midnight, and then having to leave Sunday afternoon.

Unfortunately, my drive each weekend was not what was causing her consternation... She was simply tired of the uncertainty in our lives, and she didn't care for Des Moines. She made it clear that she wasn't looking forward to her and the kids moving to Decatur. I knew things were not going well for her and this was doubly reinforced when she told me she thought she had a heart attack that week.

She told me that the previous Thursday afternoon she had severe pain across her chest, and it came on so violently that it caused her to go down to the floor. She said she could barely breathe. It apparently lasted for 3 or 4 minutes before letting up enough for her to stand up.

Are you kidding me? Because of me, her stress is so bad *it may be killing her.* As strong as Vangie was, our many moves were destroying her. After our big argument, I was overcome with guilt, self-loathing, and regret for leaving Vernal. I was acutely aware of the mess I made in Vernal, and it was eating on me worse now than ever before. I knew now I must do something because our separation issues were getting worse every week, and I didn't want to see our marriage and family completely disintegrate.

I returned to Decatur, absolutely committed to finding us a place to live. Unfortunately, the pattern of failure repeated itself. Plus, I was dealing with the stress of managing the start-up, conducting start-up meetings, verifying construction completion in the field, and learning about the plant.

One typical weekday afternoon turned into the perfect storm. I was missing Vangie and the kids terribly. I had just received a call on my office phone that a house I applied to rent was no longer available. Immediately following that, I got into an escalating, heated argument with the boiler representative about some continuously neglected deficiencies on the boiler that would delay startup. I finally had enough. In one fell swoop, something snapped in me, and I decided I simply had enough. I was done. It was time to raise the white flag and go "home" to Colorado.

I walked out of my office, got into the car, and headed for the front gate of the plant. At that singular moment I knew we had to move back to Colorado to sell cars for my brother Mike. He owned a very successful auto dealership and always left the door open to me selling cars. I knew I was done with this nomadic life. Though I was rarely depressed, I was suicidally depressed. I did not feel I could continue another moment. I was truly finished.

I uttered a simple prayer of total defeat, out-loud in the car. *"Lord, I can't go on. This isn't working. I am killing Vangie, and I need your help to get us back to Colorado and back on our feet. I can't do this any longer."* I finished the prayer and was nearing the plant exit when I heard a voice. It was *not* in my mind. *I physically heard it.* I don't expect anyone to believe this, and I don't care if you do, but I can assure you, it honestly happened.

"I have much bigger plans for you." That's all I heard. It was louder than a whisper but was very clearly a male voice. I slammed on the brakes, immediately stopped the car, and quickly turned my head side to side while looking in the back seat. There was no one in the car. I was about 50' from the stop sign by the main entrance to the plant. There was no one in front or behind me at that moment. The radio was off. Where did this clearly audible male voice come from?

I was completely shaken to my core. No one will ever convince me I did not hear this voice. Just like that time in Garden City on Mary Street when I heard the voice saying, *"It can't be stopped now."* I physically heard this voice... It is

44

unquestionable. I sat for a moment before a large truck, and another vehicle pulled up behind me, obviously wanting out of the plant. I pulled to the gate, turned onto Eldorado Street, and started driving.

I found myself on Highway 36 going south from the plant. It was a busy main thoroughfare in the area. I was still stunned by the voice and not sure what to do next. I crossed the long bridge over Lake Decatur and drove to Mt. Zion Road before realizing I couldn't just drive aimlessly. I flipped around on Mt. Zion Road and headed back on Highway 36 towards the plant.

About a mile back from Mt. Zion Road, there was a small hand-lettered sign next to the road. It was white with black letters. It simply had "HOUSE FOR RENT" and an arrow pointing down the road with "51 SADOWSKI COURT" on the bottom. I slammed on the brakes and turned onto what was East Greenfield Road and immediately turned onto Sadowksi Court and drove about a block.

There it was… *Our new rental.* It was a newer, two-story home with a two-car garage on a cul-de-sac. The area was a modern, tree-lined street, and the house looked great from the outside. I jumped out of the car and knocked on the door with no answer.

Looking through the windows revealed it was void of furniture. I wrote down the phone number on the sign in front of the house and immediately drove back to the plant as quickly as I could and called the phone number. A woman with a pleasant voice answered on the third ring.

"Hello."

"Hi, my name is Mark Gregg, and I am calling about the house for rent at 51 Sadowski Court."

45

"What can I tell you about the house?" Came the feminine reply.

"How much per month, and how soon before we can move in?"

There was a pause. She pensively replied, "The rent is $750.00 per month, and it is immediately available, but we require you to fill out an application for our evaluation."

"Where can I get the application, and can I do it right now?"

"Yes, that would be fine." Her voice lowered a bit. "I must forewarn you that we require the first month's rent, last month's rent, and a $1,000.00 damage deposit out-front."

This was a lot of money in 1988. I could tell by her voice that she was halfway expecting me to eliminate myself from consideration.

"Ma'am, I am an Engineer working for Burns and McDonnell Engineering. We designed the new powerplant being put into service at the Staley plant on Eldorado Street. I desperately need to find a place for my wife, three children, and me. I can supply you with references and have no problem with the financial requirements."

I realized I was pleading with her. It didn't matter. I knew I had to get this house.

"Please do not rent this house to anyone until I can convince you that we will take perfect care of it just as if it were our own. We will pay the rent on time and be good neighbors in the neighborhood."

"That sounds great." She answered in a more upbeat voice. "We are definitely interested in talking to you, we just need your application."

We talked for a few more minutes, and she gave me the address of their new home. Sadowski Court was their old home and was now an investment property for them.

I drove north of Decatur to their new home. It was quite an elegant property. I was met at the door by her husband. An hour later... *We had a home in Decatur.* I wrote them a check for the first and last month's rent and the damage deposit. I pulled away from their house with the keys and a document providing information for putting the utilities into our name.

It turns out they had just put the sign up less than an hour before I saw it. Make anything you want of this, but don't discount it. It happened as written. Had I not left the plant as I did and then turned around on Mt. Zion Road, I am certain I would have never seen the sign.

I bought a cheap sleeping bag and stayed at the house the rest of the week. The floor wasn't comfortable, but it was now our new home. I arranged for a moving company to come to the house in Des Moines as soon as possible to move us to Decatur.

Unfortunately, Vangie never saw Decatur or her new abode prior to 'move-in' day. She and the kids' first impression was, *"Decatur STINKS!"*

Granted, it did stink. Locals called it "the smell of money." Between AGM and Staley, there were areas of town that would instantly initiate your gag reflex. I became accustomed to it from working at the plant. Vangie and the kids never did. The odors from the multitude of food and

47

alcohol production processes were overwhelming at times. Crossing the viaduct built over the Decatur plant could absolutely gag you depending on the time of day and wind direction. All of this didn't matter... We had a home now, and we were together again.

We quickly settled into the new house and learned our way around Decatur. The first major business at hand was Church. We picked Maranatha Assembly of God for our first Sunday together in Decatur. It was a wonderful Church. The worship was amazing, the programs for the kids were great, and we enjoyed the preaching by Pastor Lowery. He and his wife, Rosemary, were the founding Pastors and did an excellent job. This became our Church home.

Unfortunately, Brandi had a difficult time adjusting to her new school. We were beginning to see that our nomadic lifestyle was problematic for her. Brittanie adjusted a little quicker, and Josh began Kindergarten in Decatur. It was during his first week that Vangie realized she may have made a serious and amusing error with Joshua.

Vangie had always referred to his private parts as his *"McGregor."* She grew up in a home with five sisters and no brothers and did not have another reference, so she simply made this up. No problem, right?

It turns out that Joshua had a classmate named Brody McGregor in his kindergarten class. When Josh first heard the boy's name, he apparently got very wide-eyed and asked the boy, "Why did they name you *that*?"

He had the same conversation with Vangie that night. It was difficult to keep a straight face as we explained that maybe we should call his genitalia something different. Live and learn. Parenting has its pitfalls.

48

Decatur was mostly a blur due to the activity at the plant. Vangie and the kids did not completely hate it but certainly did not love it. The schools were mediocre, and the crime was high. Add to this the stench that could accompany a simple drive across town, and it didn't win any popularity awards in the Gregg household. It was, overall, a turbulent time for us.

CHAPTER 6
THE STALEY CONUNDRUM

The rich and colorful history of the A.E. Staley company is emblematic of the ornate and aristocratic "Castle of the Cornfields" that was the headquarters of the A.E. Staley company (shown below).

"The Kernel and the Bean: The 75-Year Story of the Staley Company" is a good read, detailing the meager beginnings of this company and how Gene Staley built a world-class grain milling and food product operation.

Castle of the Corn Fields

The picture below is a modern photo of the corporate headquarters of the former A.E. Staley company. It is the former headquarters because a company called Tate and Lyle from England purchased the A.E. Staley company in the late 1980s.

This massive icon was originally inaugurated in 1930. Unfortunately, I only had one excursion into this building when I worked there, but it was truly a memorable and ostentatious display of early American wealth and progress.

Something I find very interesting is A.E. (Gene) Staley dedicated this monument of human endeavor "to the loyalty and faithfulness of the workers—the men and women who helped to make it a reality." This same man who dedicated the "castle of the cornfields" to the hard work of his employees

50

also had this to say when asked how many people worked at the A.E. Staley Company; He looked at the reporter and wryly said, *"About half."* This was certainly my experience in the 15 months I spent at this facility.

Prior to the new cogeneration plant being finished, someone in high places at Staley reasoned that everyone has the same wants, needs, and desires, and virtually everyone is honest, especially when subject to peer pressure. They decided that building the new, high-tech cogeneration plant was the perfect test bed to implement this new-age philosophy of management.

Because they had an existing 1930s vintage power plant filled with union employees, they would use this group to prove the new concept. They were hopeful it would ultimately eliminate union/management tensions. The first thing they did was set up extensive training for the employees moving to the new cogeneration plant.

This training apparently taught them how to be honest, upright, diligent, and industrious icons of this contemporary management style. Unfortunately, they failed to take a few things into account. Things like greed, laziness, personality schisms, and apathetic, self-centered half-wits. Don't misread me here. There were some excellent workers in the bunch. As Gene Staley bluntly stated many years prior, *"about half."*

Dave Hanson was convinced this completely hands-off management style would work. He trusted that everyone coming from the old power plant would do the right thing under every circumstance. If they hit an obstacle they couldn't solve on their own, he would intervene as a "resource" and not a supervisor.

All the vendor representatives for Foxboro, ABB, Riley, Burns, and McDonnell, etc., etc., were "resources." No one was boss. *There were no overlords here.*

If one of the union personnel was cheating on their timesheet, peer pressure would shame them into doing what was correct. If someone needed time off, they peacefully worked out the scheduling among themselves and ensured the shift(s) were covered.

What a crock of crap! From the day I arrived until the day I left, I witnessed the greedy, troublemaking jerks overwhelming the generally honest and well intentioned workers who finally succumbed to their tactics.

It was akin to what you see at a modern airport departure gate. The gate agents continuously request people to remain seated until their seating priority is called. Yet, the moment anyone starts boarding, the bulk of the people immediately jump up and get in line to ensure they beat others in their group. This is similar to what happened at the cogen plant.

As soon as one person began taking liberties with the rules, it was just a matter of time before they all did it. In fairness, some appeared to stay honest, but the ones who weren't made it very difficult for everyone else.

Sadly, a few of the individuals did not even have the aptitude or intelligence to do the job. One of the operators was nicknamed "Magilla the Gorilla." He was a perfect example. Built like a professional wrestler or a cliché cartoon strongman, he had huge shoulders, a slender waist, muscular appendages, and was a picturesque specimen of a human male.

His head was shaved, and he never said much. He generally just stared at you suspiciously and would occasionally mumble something, usually incoherent. This is not embellished. This man was exactly as I described. He was one of the operators I had to work with during the commissioning of this plant. I learned early in the start-up that he would never be an operator.

ABB had just finished the high-pressure hydraulic fluid flushes for the turbine hydraulic system. We decided to keep the system in service to continuously filter the oil. Contaminated hydraulic oil can cause unending problems with the turbine control system.

The flushes took several days, so Magilla and several other operators were involved with the process and knew what was happening. I was working in the control room with the DCS representative when Magilla entered my area and lumbered over to me.

He eyed me for a few moments and then edged up to me and in a low, menacing voice, said, "Hey, you, I gotta question." We had already worked together several times without incident. He knew what my name was.

"What's going on?" I asked, looking directly at him.

"Is that hydraulic pump for the turbine supposed to be squirting in the air?" He was completely deadpan and emotionless.

"What do you mean, squirting in the air?" I replied quickly, slightly taken aback.

"It's squirting into the air." He paused and squinted tightly. "I think it's hitting a beam on the ceiling."

At this same moment an alarm squeeled on the Foxboro system. The operator responsible for the console looked up and yelled over to me, "It is turbine low hydraulic fluid level!"

"Trip the turbine hydraulic pumps!" I hollered back to him.

I then barked, "Follow me!" as I sprinted out of the control room and down to the turbine hydraulic pumps. There was hydraulic fluid *everywhere*. It was dripping off the beams, running onto the floor and into the floor drains which is a huge issue.

"Why didn't you call the control room when you saw it was leaking?" I yelled angrily at him.

"I didn't know if it was supposed to do that. I ain't never worked around this high-tech shit before." He seemed completely sincere as he replied to me.

I couldn't believe what just happened. I also couldn't figure out whether he was being malicious or if he was truly that stupid. Why would someone act this way? Future interactions proved that he had issues far beyond reasonable repair. However, in some ways, he was still better than a few of the others. How did these people ever get hired?

One of the operators was a slick-haired psychopath named Lew Billings. He greased his hair straight back with enough oil to hold it tight to his head. This was coupled with a thin, black mustache that rimmed his upper lip. He used enough hair oil each day to top off the missing hydraulic fluid system.

Lew was always brooding and seemed to constantly yearn for confrontation. When something, no matter how insignificant, didn't go his way, he would fly off the handle into a violent rage, complete with screaming, obscenities, and threats. It was scary to watch because his face turned crimson red, as he lost total control. He would usually throw small objects like keys, pens, or pencils while on a rampage.

Later in the start-up, he would come to work on the night shift and go straight to the logic room, lying down and sleeping the remainder of the night. The Riley boiler representative and I alone, did the steam blows when he was on shift. He had no interest in being involved with the startup. In fact, he had no interest in running the plant or helping with anything.

According to the operators, he continually cheated on his time sheets. We were all afraid to say anything to him because he seemed to be a certifiable psychopath. I mentioned his behavior to Dave Hanson on two different occasions and Dave would look at me and, with total seriousness say, "Don't be concerned, he will come around. This system will work. It just needs some time."

Then there was Steve Renner. I liked Steve. He was an outspoken Christian. This did not bother me because I saw the Lord work far too many times to question Christianity. Unfortunately, Steve read a book by a man named Edgar C. Whisenant.

Edgar was a former NASA engineer and Bible student who predicted the rapture (supernatural snatching away) of the Christian Church. He indicated in the book that it would occur in 1988, sometime between September 11th and September 13th. The book was entitled 88 Reasons Why the Rapture Will Be in 1988.

Steve gave me a copy of this book, and I read it. It had some salient points. Unfortunately, Steve forgot the words of Christ, who said, "But about that day or hour no one knows, not even the angels in heaven, nor the Son, but only the Father." (Quoted from the New International Version of the Bible.)

Steve began giving away all his possessions. Early in September, Steve walked away from his high-paying job at Staley. I never saw or heard from him again. He had a wife and children that I never met, but I can't imagine how they all felt when the rapture failed to happen as predicted.

Another distinctive individual I worked with at the cogen plant was Billy Corder. He was about twice my age and the oldest operator in the cogen plant. He was relatively sharp and very experienced in the operation of the old power plant that the cogen was replacing. I liked him even though he tended to be a sarcastic, sharp-tongued realist.

He loathed the new management style, but he truly knew how to work hard and wanted to do a decent job. Unfortunately, he struggled to move from the 1930s technology of the old stoker-fired power complex to the massively new technology of the cogen plant.

Billy felt the new management style was an abomination from hell that would fail miserably. He was correct in his assessment of its failure. He was also very frustrated because he was doing things the right way and not cheating on his time sheet or gaming the system like several of the others. Though he was vocal about those who were cheating and abusing the system, it appeared that peer pressure did not influence the cheating workers. They would simply insult him to his face and continue with their misdeeds.

There were several other operators that were problematic in one or more ways. However, the biggest problem at that time was the plant itself. There were serious issues with the new Foxboro I/A system. It was designed to be self-troubleshooting. There were application processors (AP) and control processors (CP). The processor health was relegated to a green LED (everything good) or a red LED (processor failed). When something failed in a processor, the red LED was supposed to illuminate. The technician needs only to find the AP or CP that had a red light and replace it with a new one. At least, that's how it was supposed to work.

We were continuously experiencing "GREEN DEATH," as the Foxboro engineers called it. The CP or AP would fail, and yet the light would stay green. The problem was overwhelming in the first several months of the start-up. Each "GREEN DEATH" experience would shut the control system down, causing huge issues.

The two fluidized bed boilers being constructed by Riley provided one delay after another. There were extensive boiler design issues and even some design issues with the plant auxiliaries. The first boiler feed pump we put into service turned into quite a thrill ride.

I walked the entire feedwater system down to check for completion numerous times. We waited for the Ingersoll Rand representative to be on-site for the initial start of the three 50% capacity boiler feed pumps.

When the moment came for the first pump to start, I rechecked the alignment of the valves, ensured everything was filled, and made certain the pump was ready to start. I ensured everyone involved was versed in what they were supposed to do. The relatively large boiler feed pumps sat on the northeast corner of the bottom floor next to a large overhead door.

I keyed the mic on my radio and clearly called out, "Control room, please start 1-A boiler feed pump!" The motor immediately whined in defiance as the pump screamed up to 3600 RPM. A few seconds before the rated speed was achieved… ***BLAAAAAAAAAM!***

There was a water hammer so intense it shook the entire plant and tore the recirculation line off its hangers! The shock of the water hammer instantly caused everyone, including me, to sprint for the open overhead door to get away from the calamity at hand.

I immediately screamed into the radio, "TRIP THE BOILER FEED PUMP! TRIP THE BOILER FEED PUMP! TRIP THE BOILER FEED PUMP!!!" The pump rolled down to a stop in a matter of seconds.

I glanced at the Ingersoll Rand representative. His face was ashen, and his eyes were wide open. My knees were knocking as I was momentarily shaken by the shock of the water hammer. I had experienced many, many water hammers in my career to this point, but none were as unexpected as this one. Everything was checked multiple times and aligned properly.

We analyzed the entire situation while having construction repair the piping. We could not find a reason for the hammer to occur. A few days later, we attempted another start. The same thing happened. We were a little more prepared this time, but it was still unnerving.

I had to bring in Bob Hellman, the Burns and McDonnell engineer who designed the system's piping. He redesigned the piping with breakdown orifices, costing us several weeks.

During this time, Staley hired a contract electrical and controls engineer named Arnie Gaines. Arnie was small and fit, and he always had a friendly smile on his face. He was in

58

his early 30s and seemed to really know his stuff. He was brought in due to issues with interfacing programmable logic controllers (PLCs) with the Foxboro DCS system.

Arnie and I hit it off the very first day he worked there. He had a sense of humor compatible with mine and seemed to be a great guy. He was well-received at the plant because he was generally cheerful and viewed as knowledgeable in his craft.

One reason Arnie stood out to me was because virtually everyone at the plant used extensive vulgarity. It was just the way things were in these plants. However, Arnie kept his mouth clean and avoided as much profanity as possible. This was one of many items that drew us together.

After working together for a couple of weeks, we began talking on a more personal level. Arnie was a Christian and had a wife named Joyce and two young children, a boy and a girl. Joyce was a construction electrician and worked at the AGM cogeneration plant. It was the largest cogeneration plant of its kind in the United States and was under construction in Decatur at the same time as the Staley plant. He appeared to be happily married and appeared to love his kids very much. All these things helped us to form a bond with one another.

About three weeks into our working relationship, Arnie arrived at the plant several hours late. It was a Monday morning, and he was unshaven, had large, puffy bags under his eyes, and looked haggard. His clothes were soiled and unclean, as if he had slept in them for a couple of days. He barely looked up as he came into the control room, dropping hard into his chair.

His 'office' was nothing more than a fold-up table in the control room that he worked from when he wasn't out in the plant. He appeared to just be sitting there with his head partially down.

I walked over, sliding a chair next to his. "How's it going today?" I asked pensively.

He never looked up. "Not good." He mumbled quietly. That was it… No explanation, no eye contact.

"Is there something I can do?"

"I don't think anyone can do anything." He was still mumbling and looking down. "I don't know what to do now." He sniffled. It seemed like he was weeping, but I couldn't see his face clear enough to tell.

"Please tell me what's wrong… Maybe I can help." I was truly concerned and startled at his appearance.

The legs of his chair screeched as he angrily pushed it back. "No one can do anything. It is done, it is f%$#ing over." He stood up and started towards the control room door. Though he tried to turn his head to hide it, I could tell he was crying. I was shocked at his profanity. He NEVER used those words.

I followed him out of the control room and onto the turbine deck. He stopped and stood at the southeast corner by an extraction valve. I approached slowly. He was leaning forward with his arms outstretched on an I-beam, staring at the wall, and was now openly sobbing.

As I approached, he shook his head and said, "I tried to end it all last night, but I am too damn cowardly to pull the trigger."

I was stunned and shocked to my core. "Arnie, what in the heck is going on?" I pleaded.

"Joyce cheated on me." He continued to stare at the wall while shaking his head.

"How do you know?" I asked skeptically.

"She told me!" He turned dark and angry. "She came home from work Friday night and told me she had sex with another construction worker, RIGHT AT THE DAMN PLANT!" He stiffened and jutted his jaw. "What kind of tramp did I marry??? She had sex in a circuit-breaker room on the floor like a dog in heat."

I was stunned beyond all measure. How do you console someone under these circumstances, especially when he always talks about how wonderful she was?

"Has something like this ever happened before?" I asked carefully, not sure what to say.

"Who knows? Until last night I thought we had a GREAT marriage."

"Does she want a divorce?" I asked tentatively.

"No, she actually had the gall to tell me she felt horrible, and it was impulse sex and not meaningful." He paused and, with total angst, said, "I don't even know who she is... Or, for that matter, what she is."

It struck me as odd that she would come home and tell him about her indiscretion. Without knowing her, I was unsure what to think. I was still agonizing over him saying he didn't have the guts to pull the trigger. I knew I needed to intervene in some way.

"Arnie, you have two kids that need BOTH you and Joyce. If she had the guts to tell you it was a one-time indiscretion and she felt terrible about it, why wouldn't you believe her?" I put my hand on his shoulder and continued. "Arnie, I don't know Joyce, but it sounds like she made a horrible mistake but chose not to hide it. Maybe you should cut her some slack, if for nothing else, for the sake of the kids?"

He began to sob again. "I just don't know what to do."

With my hand on his shoulder, I lowered my head and prayed loud enough he could hear me. "Father, in the name of Jesus, I pray that right now you touch Arnie and Joyce and bring about a spirit of peace and forgiveness on both of them and their marriage. I don't know the details, but I do know they both need you and need your love, peace, and comfort right now. Please intervene in their lives. I ask this in Jesus's name, AMEN."

Arnie just stared at me blankly for a moment before saying, "Thanks, Mark. I appreciate this more than you know."

We talked a bit longer and then went back into the control room. I invited him to dinner that night. He declined, saying he was going to try to go back home and talk to Joyce. He had stormed out of the house on Friday evening and had been living in his pick-up since then and had not talked to her since he left.

He went home that afternoon and got some clothes, and moved out of his house. Some nights, he would stay in a motel; others, he would stay in his pickup. I couldn't convince him to stay with us. He just kept saying he didn't want to be a bother.

The next two weeks found us together almost continuously. He started coming to the house in the evenings, and we would go to the basement and talk there. We discussed the whole situation from every conceivable angle, always using a Biblical perspective. I was worried he was going to try and do away with himself again. However, he seemed to be over that for now.

One evening, he told me that Joyce wanted to get counseling. When he told me this, I decided to be straight with him on my beliefs about divorce.

"Arnie, I am going to be honest with you." I was trying to keep things measured because I did not want to seem accusatory. "I think 95% of all divorces are the man's fault, and I think that selfishness is the primary cause."

"Why would you say that?" He asked angrily.

"Think about it. If a marriage has financial trouble, it is probably because of selfishness from one or both of the parties. A lack of money does not intrinsically cause a fight between spouses, it is the desire of one or the other to spend money they don't have that causes the fight. In other words, selfishness."

He started to object, "Yeah, but…"

I cut him off mid-sentence. "They say sex issues are a major cause of marital problems, but I say it is selfishness that manifests itself in sexual situations that cause marital problems." I pointed to the Bible. "It gives a lot of rules about how husband and wives should conduct themselves regarding sex and even says the wife's body is not hers, but his, and his body is hers."

With this, he drew back and retorted, "Are you really blaming what happened on me?"

"No." I replied quickly. "I am saying in some form or fashion it is selfishness. In my opinion there has never been a divorce that was not ultimately caused by selfishness on one or both parts." I paused for a moment. "Think about it. Think about every cause of a divorce there could be. Let's just say one party gets sick, like cancer or something. If the other party feels they can't deal with this, it is selfishness on their part." He stared at me for a minute but didn't say anything. I could tell he was thinking about what I just said.

I continued. "What if you were injured and couldn't have sex with her? If she cheated, it would be selfishness on her part. However, it has been my experience that the few times I have heard about marriages where one could no longer have sex due to physical reasons, the other accepted it, and the marriage continued. However, in marriages where one just doesn't want sex, the other gets mad and cheats."

He brooded for a moment. "You are definitely saying it is my fault, aren't you?"

"Arnie, I have absolutely no idea whose fault it is that Joyce cheated on you. I just know that she told you about it the day it happened, and she told you she felt terrible about it. I also know she is asking you to go to counseling with her." I then looked him straight in the eyes. "Go get counseling with your wife and *fix this*. All I ever heard from you prior to the incident was how amazing she was. Why did this suddenly change? Why did she tell you about it? I don't know what caused her to cheat, but it is probably something very complex that ends in selfishness on her part or your part. Get some counseling with your wife and fix this!"

He looked at me like a deer caught in headlights. "Mark, I have to leave. I will see you tomorrow at work." Without another word, he jumped up and left. I was distraught because I didn't know if I did good or bad. I was leaning towards bad.

The next day, he came into work, pulled me aside, and said, "I moved back home, and we are getting a marriage counselor."

Arnie remained at home and they attended Christian marriage counseling. They remained married and eventually had several more children. The last time I talked to him, many years later, they were still very happy together. This didn't end things between us. Arnie and I were still not finished with each other yet.

CHAPTER 7

FINALLY, ANOTHER DREAM

The cogen plant start-up proceeded agonizingly slow. As the start-up lagged, Dave Hanson and I were forced to split the management duties. He worked from 7:00 AM till 7:00 PM every **DAY,** and I worked from 7:00 PM till 7:00 AM every **NIGHT**. No days off, no reprieve. I hated night shifts worse than a hog hates a sausage factory. I was constantly exhausted and grumpy, and I was a miserable husband, father, and person.

Sleep was fleeting, and depression was slipping in. Once again, I was questioning the life choices that led to this situation. The fact that I had not had another prophetic dream in over six years occasionally bothered me. Why did they stop? I was still the same, right? Yet there had not been any repeat of the earlier dreams that were clearly from the Lord. Things were about to change in a big way.

The next dream happened on a Wednesday. I was sleeping fitfully that afternoon prior to going into the plant for my night shift. This dream was completely different than the dreams I experienced many years earlier. In the prior dreams, I would sometimes see something insignificant that would happen verbatim the next day, and then I would see the far-reaching purpose of the dream.

This dream was probably more of a vision because I was at least *partially* awake. There were only two words spoken and no other sound. I was standing in a room teaching and felt this incredible all-encompassing presence. It was felt, not seen, but I was at ease. I looked out into the classroom, but it seemed as if I was looking across the entire world. There seemed to be vast distances between the students.

I had a large computer monitor in front of me and I noticed my students had computer monitors in front of them also. We were communicating, but no words were being spoken. It was then that I heard the only two audible words in the entire dream/vision.

"Build this." The words echo in my heart to this day. *"Build this."*

I became acutely aware that I was teaching through the monitors in the dream. Unlike the previous dreams, I did not have any apparent 'proof' that it was from the Lord. There was only one thing presented to me, and it was truly ethereal. I felt completely at ease even though I didn't really understand what I was supposed to do other than *"build this."*

I continued to lay in bed and pray for a bit before falling soundly asleep. Vangie had to wake me to ensure I made it to work on time. This was very unusual because I was usually awake hours before having to leave.

I didn't tell her right away about the dream because there was so little to say. The only words were *"build this."* I thought about it the entire night at work and knew I had to do something.

Arnie Gaines appeared to have decent programming skills, so I didn't leave the plant the next morning until after he arrived. After Dave Hanson relieved me, I pulled Arnie aside and told him about the dream.

When I was done, I asked, "Do you want to help me build some kind of computer-based training for the utility industry?"

"Uhhh, okay, *sure*...?" He then smiled. "Do you have any idea how you are going to do this?" He appeared skeptical.

"Not at this moment, but it only makes sense. It is 1988. Computers are taking over everything. *Why not training?*"

He looked at me thoughtfully and then nodded his head and smiled. "I would absolutely like to be involved if you can put together an idea and a game plan that makes sense!"

There you have it. *All I had to do was design a system to train people remotely using computers, and the rest would be easy.* Arnie's words, along with the "***build this***" dream, resonated in my sleep-deprived, pea-sized brain for the next several days.

It is important to note that Microsoft Windows didn't exist yet. This means that PowerPoint or other presentation software had not been developed. Apple had a much more intuitive interface, but the non-Apple computers were still working from the clunky, difficult-to-use, command-line-based DOS operating system.

After a few days of rumination, I arrived at what I thought was a workable system. It would, of course, use some kind of modem and phone lines. It would entail a split screen format that would display training material on the top half of the display and interactive feedback on the bottom half of the display. I would customize this to a client's needs and respond to the students individually.

There you have it. This proved how stupid I am. Seriously, the pitfalls with this idea are massive, glaring, and time-consuming. My thought was to go to a plant and sell them a training *"subscription"* that was personalized and inexpensive. I would then develop a massive amount of training that could be presented via a split display while responding to questions and comments on the interactive part of the display as they came in. Heck, there is barely any labor involved with this debacle.

I presented my plan to Arnie. He was not a visionary as much as he was an industrious programmer and computer guru. When I explained how I thought this would work, he loved it. His next comment was classic; "Mark, how will I get reimbursed for building the software to make this work?" He was wide-eyed and seemed excited about being involved with this conceptual idea.

I thought about it for a few moments and then pensively asked him, "Would you be interested in having a percentage of ownership in this concept?"

Arnie never flinched. "I would rather let you own 100% and just get paid an hourly rate for my software development services. I have a ton of bills right now." He paused and, in an upbeat manner, added, "Plus, this way, you would own the finished product."

Okay, readers, pay attention... If you ever come up with an amazing idea and people say they want to be a part of it but ***NOT*** hold any ownership, it is probably because they think the idea absolutely stinks but do not want to hurt your feelings.

I was a bit surprised Arnie was not interested in ownership. My plan was to trade an ownership share for some of the up-front work. Arnie's idea was to relieve my wallet of excess cash for an idea that was quite stupid. I would figure this out, but not until I gave Arnie a fair amount of money. I don't believe for a moment that Arnie was being malicious.

He was willing to support the effort but not for the blue sky and promises.

It took a couple of weeks before Arnie presented me with a working system that provided a split screen, allowing two-way communication on the bottom portion of the display while allowing me to put simple graphics and text on the top portion of the display.

In those days, we were working almost entirely with either monochrome green displays or amber displays. There were CGA color displays and even a few higher-resolution color displays at that time, but they were extremely expensive.

I contacted Bob Culligan, my ex-plant manager when I was in Vernal, Utah. He was now at the Hugo Plant in Oklahoma. I asked if he would be interested in previewing this new concept.

After explaining it in detail, he bluntly said, "I have no interest in this. It doesn't sound efficient, and you would have to be an expert on our plant or whatever plant that you would sell it to." He paused to soften the blow. "Good luck with your concept, I wish you the best." Essentially all he said was, *"Don't call me, I will call you."*

I realized this format was not going to work. What I needed was a presentation software product that allowed me to storyboard a concept or topic over as many pages as necessary that incorporated text, graphics, and even some animation. It's too bad PowerPoint was not available in 1988. However, I started thinking there must be something already developed that can be used right out of the box.

Delving into this subject, I found a few presentation programs available that appeared to fill the need. A couple of them were very expensive, and the owners had to be paid royalties for anything you built with their product. This incensed me.

They were saying that if I buy their tools and then expend my labor to build a presentation, I still must pay them a percentage of anything that I sold, even though it was my labor that built the finished product. This was unacceptable to me, and I wouldn't even consider it.

The problem was a simple one. The best tools all required royalty payments. However, I wanted something that did not require royalties. From the Computer Shopper magazine, I found a product called PC Pilot. It was a code generator for DOS-based systems that did basically what I wanted. It was cheap and required no royalties.

I called the owner and ordered it. You get what you pay for. It was code intensive, regardless of how it was billed. I was not a programmer, so I needed something that did not require extensive coding (programming) knowledge or capabilities. I called Larry Kheriaty, the developer of PC Pilot, and asked if he knew of another product that required less coding.

Turns out he was a computer science professor at Western Washington University in Bellingham, Washington. He had an associate professor who built an interface for PC Pilot called PROPI. I bought it. It appeared to do what I wanted to do.

PROPI (PRO-PIE) allowed the user to build storyboards using graphics and bitmap pictures. It contained basic logic operators that allowed you to ask questions and score the answers. Everything had to be multiple-choice, but this was not a major issue.

I began building a basic powerplant training fundamentals module at the plant. I justified doing it on Staley's time because I used it to help train their operators at no additional charge other than my salary. As I showed my minimal progress to the operators, they seemed to like it. They thought it was a novel method of training.

Though I was contracted directly with Burns and McDonnell, Steve Swain was still handling my pay and some of the interactions with Burns. However, he went to work with Ogden Martin Systems. Ogden Martin was quickly developing into a juggernaut in the refuse-to-energy business. Steve went to work for them as their manager of new plant commissioning.

I sent Steve Swain a snippet of the computer-based training fundamentals I was doing on a 3.5" diskette. He was impressed enough with the computer-based training product that he gave me the contact information for John Collier, a corporate manager at Ogden Martin Systems.

I, of course, didn't know it then, but they would eventually become our very first sale of Computer Based Training (CBT). A sale that came at a very unexpected and opportune season. Besides being our first sale, they also became a major contributor to the development effort. It was odd the way it unfolded.

CHAPTER 8
OGDEN MARTIN

It took several attempts to reach the elusive John Collier. His secretary was obviously screening his calls and didn't seem very interested in letting me speak to him. I left several messages with her to no avail. I told Steve Swain about this. He suggested I be patient as John was an extremely busy man and he would probably return my call at some point.

It was a few weeks after this that John contacted me.

"Mr. Gregg, this is John Collier of Ogden Martin Systems."

I didn't waste words, jumping right into my reason for talking to him.

"John, I have a new technical training concept that I would like to share with you. It uses personal computers to provide training for your plant operators. It allows them to train at their own pace, and it provides electronic exams with remediation and permanent record keeping, ensuring they are completing the training. It is *extremely* cost-effective."

He was quick to reply. "We need training, but our budgets are very, very minimal..." He turned away from the phone, and I could hear him talking to someone else. He obviously covered the mouthpiece, but I could tell he wasn't listening to me. After a brief conversation with someone else, he returned to the line with me. "Anyway, if what you have is inexpensive and works, I would at least be interested in looking at it."

73

I thought quickly before answering him. "Because it is in the early stages of development, it will be very cost-effective for you." I gulped a breath and continued. "If I could have an opportunity to show it to you, I think you would be impressed."

"Fine. Can you be at the Indianapolis Refuse to Energy plant next Tuesday at 0900 hours?"

I didn't expect this in any way. "Uh, yes, that would work for me. Can I get the address of the facility?" He was again talking with someone else near him. This time, he didn't even cover the mouthpiece. It was obvious that it had nothing to do with me or our call.

"What's that?" He came back and asked with some annoyance in his voice. I wasn't sure if he was talking to me or to the other person he was conversing with.

"Could I get the address of the plant?" I again asked.

"I will have Marge call you with the details." He then hung up the phone without even saying goodbye. I didn't think that being in an upper management position excused rudeness, but I was clearly ignorant.

Fortunately, his secretary called a bit later and provided the address of the plant in Indianapolis. She was also a bit terse, but I got what I needed from her and she even said "goodbye" when the call was over.

Because I was a contractor and had not taken any time off while working continuous nightshifts, I didn't ask Dave Hanson for a few days off. I simply told him at shift turnover that evening that I could not be there Monday and Tuesday of the next week. He was taken aback by my declaration but accepted it with his typical goofy smile. I could have told him

I was murdering my wife during those days and would have still received the same dopey smile.

DOS-based laptop computers were just coming onto the scene in 1988. They were large, heavy, expensive, and either grayscale, green, or amber monochrome displays. Therefore, I had to take a large CPU and a large, heavy monitor to Indianapolis. I splurged and purchased a 19" EGA monitor (the forerunner to VGA) so that the system would show well.

I already designed the curriculum for what I now call *The Power Fundamentals* training system. It would ultimately include 14 'modules' of CBT. The first module was *Introduction to Power Generation*. It was a simple primer with minor animations and illustrations.

It was a read-only system as audio production was still not a common man's reality. Essentially, it was an electronic page-turner that had exams built into it. The exams had to be passed with a minimum score before they could move to the

next chapter in a module. Simple, but at the time, still new and exciting because using a computer for training was considered cutting edge in 1988.

Vangie and I took the kids with us to Indianapolis. It was a three-hour drive, and we needed some family time. We checked into a Holiday Inn with an indoor swimming pool

Indianapolis Refuse to Energy Facility

75

Monday afternoon and swam with the kids and had a great time. We went to dinner together and spent the evening enjoying this rare family time.

Tuesday morning, I arrived at the plant at about 7:30 to give me ample time to set up the computer and be ready for John to view the course in its currently completed form.

The exterior of the Indianapolis Refuse to Energy plant looked like a conventional power plant. It had a tall boiler building with what looked like a shorter, broad turbine room on the front. Unfortunately, the steam turbine was actually in a small, dark room in the bowels of the plant. The part that, from the outside, looked like the turbine room was called the *tipping floor*. This is where the large garbage trucks would drive in and dump their municipal waste.

The smell of the tipping room would quickly and effectively induce a total gag reflex. They even sprayed air fresheners to try and suppress the putrescent smell of rotting garbage. It was *beyond* repulsive. I don't know how the workers could stand to work in that area.

After setting up the computer in a conference room and going through the first module, I was satisfied that it was ready, but I was still incredibly nervous. The CBT I had completed to-date showed well but was still a bit 'buggy'. If it locked during the demo, I was probably screwed. It locked once on me while testing. It took about 3 or 4 minutes to reboot and return to where I was when it locked. I prayed intensely that this would not happen during the presentation.

9:00 came and went. There was no sign of John Collier. He must have hit some traffic. 10:00 came and went. Still no John Collier. My nerves were now shot. No one came into the conference room to update me, so at about 10:30, I went to the plant receptionist.

"Do you know if John Collier is still coming to this presentation?"

She seemed distant and aloof as she said, "All I know is I had a message that the conference room was reserved for a presentation this morning. I have no idea where John would be." She then added with a caustic tone, "John doesn't work from here. We almost never see him."

I returned to the conference room antsy, nervous, and fidgety. I decided to call his phone and see if his secretary would update me on the situation. As I approached the receptionist's desk to see if I could use a phone, John walked in with three other men. I wouldn't have known who it was, but the receptionist greeted him by name and then pointed him to me.

"Mr. Collier, I set this gentleman up in the conference room for your meeting." She then turned to me. "I'm sorry. What is your name again?"

"Mark Gregg."

John aggressively approached me with his right hand outstretched. "Mark, sorry for being late. Several things came up this morning. I only have a few minutes to look at your product. Let's get this done."

Wow! I was thrown for a loop. We went immediately to the conference room. He then quickly introduced his minions that were following him and then said, "Give me the Cliff Notes version of your presentation. I have *exactly* five minutes." There was no apology for the tardiness. In fact, his demeanor honestly made me feel like I should apologize to him. Everything I originally planned to say was now out the window.

I quickly showed him how the system required logging in and then rapidly pounded through several pages to the first exam. While answering the multiple-choice exam questions, I told him if I did not get at least 70% of the questions correct, I would be forced to start over and not be allowed to progress to the next chapter until I passed.

"Can you adjust the failure percentage?" he asked tersely.

"Yes, you can set it at any percentage you want."

"How hard is it to gain access to the record files?" He was, again, very curt.

"Everything is password protected. Without a password, you cannot access the records."

"Do you have a syllabus or curriculum document you can leave with me?"

"Yes, right here." I handed him the list of the modules that I had preliminarily outlined. He quickly glanced at it.

"You indicated on the phone the system wasn't complete. How much of this list is finished?"

I knew then I was hitting an iceberg as I sheepishly said, "Only the first module, *Introduction to Power Generation,* is complete. However, we are currently working on the rest of the modules."

"You only have *ONE* module of this course complete?" he asked in an annoyed tone.

I answered as confidently as possible. "Yes, but we are working on it daily." I realized if he asked who "we" entailed,

I would have to tell him it was just me. Thankfully, he never asked.

He quickly held out his right hand and said, "Thanks for coming and demonstrating this product. We might be interested in the future. Let me know when your product is finished and ready to use."

His tone was decisive and final. After he shook my hand, he and his three minions abruptly left the room. This entire encounter took about 10 total minutes.

Initially I was crushed. However, on the drive back to the hotel I realized I arrived with a product that was less than 5% complete. If I were buying a new car, and all they could sell was the steering wheel and a spare tire, I would walk away also.

The trip wasn't a total loss. Though grossly unsuccessful, I had my first opportunity to try and sell this product. I needed the experience. Plus, as a family, we had a great time together. This was something that had been lacking due to my horrendous night shift schedule. I had no idea what the future held for the product, but I never dreamed they would end up being an integral part of it.

After returning to work in Decatur, I focused on the training system as much as possible. The plant start-up was taking increasingly more of my time, but I tried to put in as many hours on the software development as possible. I was now envisioning a world where I had an entire product to sell and not just a steering wheel or spare tire. This vision coerced and animated me to continue developing the software as aggressively as possible.

Unfortunately, both my excitement and the development progress quickly waned due to the plant start-up requiring more and more of my time. The non-stop, death-inducing, grinding, relentless, and unforgiving graveyard shifts were crushing my spirit due to sleep deprivation, and was now pushing me into the depths of depression.

I cannot over-emphasize the negative effect the graveyard shifts were having on me. This fact became quite evident to us all and climaxed during a visit from Vangie's sister.

Vangie's sister Linda and her diminutive husband, Ted, lived in Chicago. He was an Army Recruiter and a pain in the butt. Suffering extensively from 'little man syndrome,' he wasn't well-liked by any of the family members due to his extremely cocky nature and know-it-all personality.

Linda and Ted decided to drive down to Decatur to visit us. During this time, the 1988 presidential election was in full swing, and I was wound tight as a drum due to sleep deprivation, and what I saw as an inferior presidential candidate in Michael Dukakis.

Ted was probably voting for Bush, but his personality is such that he loved debate. No, not true. He loved being a total pain in the butt and generating controversy. When he realized I was voting for George Bush, he applied the full-court press for me to vote for Dukakis. He wouldn't let it drop. He did not want to discuss *ANYTHING* but the presidential election, no matter how hard I tried to change the subject.

Each time I changed the subject, he returned the focus to any issue with Dukakis that seemed to push my buttons. His entire objective was to inflame me. ***It was just Ted's way...***

I was dead-tired, trying to be a good host and putting up with his relentless crap that was becoming increasingly pointed and dogmatic when something snapped inside me. In one millisecond, I lost all control, sense, restraint, and presence of mind.

Without warning, I swung around and grabbed him by his lapel and, with both hands, slammed him against the wall as hard as I could. Adrenaline was coursing through my body. For a split second, I honestly wanted to kill him.

This occurred in the kitchen next to the door into the garage. With the entire weight of my body against him, while my left hand grasped his lapel, I threw the garage door open with my right hand and thrust him down the two steps onto the cold, hard, concrete garage floor, screaming, ***"GET THE HELL OUT OF MY HOUSE AND DON'T YOU EVER COME BACK!"***

I am not a fighter, nor trained to do so. He had been in the United States Army for years. I am certain he would have killed me. However, he was so surprised, so shocked, and so thoroughly rattled that he just sat on the garage floor for at least a minute, completely stunned. His face lost all color. I whipped around to see Linda crying and Vangie looking at me, shocked and wide-eyed. Rightfully so. I screwed-up. ***Badly***.

Ted and Linda immediately departed back to Chicago without so much as another word. As soon as they were out of the driveway, I looked dutifully at Vangie and sheepishly said, "I am so sorry. I was wrong…"

Before I could complete my planned, lengthy apology, she looked at me and said, "You did to Ted what everyone else always wanted to do. Forget it. Maybe he won't come back."

Now, it was my turn to be stunned and have a look of unbelief on my face. I knew Ted was not her favorite person but I was shocked that she told me this.

Unfortunately, as life happens, Linda and Ted were divorced a few years later, but not before Vangie had *her* turn assaulting Ted… This is another story for later. Funny how we bob and weave through life while the pieces come in and out like a gargantuan jigsaw puzzle.

Needless to say, I went to work that evening more tired than usual. The remainder of the Staley Cogen start-up was slow, painful, and episodic. Between equipment failures, design issues, and plant personnel issues, it seemed as if we would never turn this plant into an operational facility.

I did my best to stay out of trouble and provide them a pound or more of my flesh every night to ensure the plant start-up was completed as smoothly as possible. Thankfully, my efforts were recognized.

After the plant began operating, they asked if I would be interested in the Plant Superintendent's position. Why?

Dave Hanson was leaving because the social experiment of letting the foxes run the hen house failed, catastrophically. Everyone was pointing their fingers at someone else as to why this style of management failed. However, it was simple. ***There was NO management.***

Eliminating all supervisors and managers created a vacuum. Letting the union personnel do what they wanted within this vacuum produced chaos and a non-functional working environment that cost Staley millions of dollars in low productivity, producing a workforce that didn't care whether the plant ran or not. The union was not prepared nor capable of operating without pointed direction and a cattle prod to keep them moving.

One of the strongest union-mongers was an operator and Union Steward they called Tuffy. He was pugnacious, hard-nosed, but a fair and decent guy. At least, in my estimation, he was. It didn't matter what the union contract stated, he would enforce it with zeal.

We became guarded but good friends at the plant because we both knew what to expect from each other. He and I would do exactly what the union contract said, even though I hated most of it with a passion, and he knew it. Fighting against the contract was a losing proposition because, as the name suggests, it is a *contract*.

Tuffy and I continuously argued over the union contract, but the argument wasn't about its enforcement, it was about its **total** absurdity. He said this was why he liked me. *I wholly adhered to the contract* but didn't pretend it was correct or that it even made sense in many cases.

When I left Staley in early 1989, he gave me a keepsake coin from England that his grandmother gave him. He said he sincerely enjoyed working with me and earnestly wished I would reconsider the Superintendent position and remain at Staley.

A few months after we left Decatur, Staley Management locked out the union employees. It was not unanticipated. Management's eyes finally opened to the untenable morass their poorly thought-out social experiment yielded. *There was nothing to fix.* They needed to start over. As is always the case when livelihoods are lost, and unions are involved, it got ugly.

Apparently, Tuffy was outside the gate picketing with some of the other union folks when he stopped a non-union coal delivery truck and recklessly tried to pull the driver out of the seat. Unfortunately, the driver grabbed a heavy steel pipe he was carrying for this very purpose and clobbered Tuffy in the head with it. The injury was so severe that Tuffy had a major brain bleed and never fully recovered. This saddened me. *It was so preventable.*

In case you are wondering why I turned down the Operations Superintendent position (and straight dayshift), I knew the strike and lockout were coming. I viewed the plant and operations group as being wholly impossible to manage. Because of this, I certainly didn't want to literally live at the plant during the strike/lockout and then work through a massive rebuilding of the plant personnel.

Besides this, Decatur was rough around the edges and a difficult living environment that neither Vangie nor I wished to raise our kids. We decided to move to the next Burns and McDonnell project. It was providing operational and engineering support for three biomass-fired facilities in California. Life was about to make another enormous, God-directed, change for us.

CHAPTER 9
MERCED, CALIFORNIA

The move from Decatur, Illinois, to Merced, California, was a blur. We stopped in Montrose for a few days to visit both of our parents. The kids enjoyed seeing their grandparents. *We enjoyed the break from the kids while they were at the grandparents.*

During this visit I realized that after growing up in the gorgeous, picturesque Uncompahgre Valley of Colorado, I had taken for granted the rugged, snow-capped San Juan mountains.

The beauty of the area is stunning, and I never fully appreciated it until now. Gazing at the majestic Storm King Mountain, along with the staggering backdrop of the snow-capped San Juans standing as rugged sentinels reaching into the heavens induced a peace and calm beyond human understanding. I knew I could never take this area for granted again.

I so wanted to remain there, but the reality of meeting the core needs of life would override the impractical wishes and wanderings of an unsettled mind. It was time to come back to reality and move forward with our current path.

After arriving in California, we found a three-bedroom, two-bath home to rent in Merced. We did not waste any time renting it. We were sick of hotels. The search was intense, but by now, we were seasoned pros at finding a home.

Our first Sunday in Merced found us attending a Full Gospel Church. It was held in what appeared to be a warehouse but was austerely converted into a Church setting.

However, *The worship was incredible!* We arrived as the worship service was starting and sat in the very back row. Why not? We didn't know a soul, and we had the kids with us.

It didn't take long before we were captivated and elevated into the beautiful, resplendent worship enveloping the sanctuary. About 15 minutes into the service, I was drawn out of the mesmerizing presence of God by the Pastor standing right next to me. I hadn't even noticed him coming off the platform.

Arriving quietly at the back row, he reached out and placed his hand on my head, startling me. We locked eyes for a moment, and then softly, but with authority, he said, *"Thou art a worshipper. The Lord says, thou art a worshipper. The Lord would have you know that He has seen your worship and knows your heart. You must now go forth and complete that which He called you to do."*

I was staggered by his proclamation. There must have been 300 or more people in this service. I had never seen him before, and I am certain he had never seen me before. Upon completion of his prophetic utterance, he turned and quietly went back to the platform. The worship service continued for another 30 or more minutes before he began to preach.

At the completion of the service, someone came back and handed me a cassette tape of his prophecy over me. All I could think about was the two words given to me in the dream that night in Decatur... *"Build this..."* Unfortunately, I had virtually stopped working on the computer based training system. I ran out of steam due to the graveyard shifts coupled with the grueling Staley Plant start-up and now the move to Merced. The dream with the words *"Build this"* was now looming large in my heart.

That night, I prayed and prayed, asking the Lord for help completing the modules. I knew it was going to be almost impossible to complete the Power Fundamentals course while working full-time at these biomass plants as a contractor. Besides, I didn't have a clue what I was supposed to do here. All I knew was, Burns and McDonnell moved us to Merced to help a struggling, biomass-fired powerplant come to profitability. I wasn't given much more information than this. Unfortunately, it was far more complex and sinister than either of us realized.

The company I was contracting to was called CAPCO. They had two extremely small, barely operational biomass plants with a much larger third one under construction. Unbeknownst to me, there were serious financial problems and as I later learned, a ton of graft and corruption to enhance the incompetent management. Our ride in Merced was about to get very turbulent.

Merced was a relatively small town. It was near Fresno in the Central Valley area of California. According to the U.S Geological Services, the Central Valley supplies eight percent of U.S. agricultural output and **produces at least 25% of the Nation's food**, including 40% of the Nation's fruits, nuts, and other table foods.

Until you spend time there, you cannot fathom the seemingly infinite expanse of agriculture stretching hundreds of miles in every direction. Most outsiders view California through 'city-lenses' formed from endless pictures of the teeming, suburban sprawl of Los Angeles, San Francisco, and San Diego. However, at 42,000 square miles, the San Joaquin and Sacramento Valleys are an agricultural mecca about *the size of the entire state of Tennessee.*

For decades, it was common practice to burn agricultural land to clean bio-waste from farms and fields. The sheer amount of smoke and haze produced by countless, massive agricultural burns was staggering. To help eliminate this, the California state government provided substantial tax incentives for companies to build power plants fueled by this substantial biological waste. These biomass plants were touted as incredible money-makers. Besides huge tax incentives, the "fuel" was free, and the plants would sell their electricity on the open market.

This was supposed to be a win-win-win equation for everyone. The plants were required to burn the field waste cleanly, while capturing the majority of particulate and volatile pollution, substantially cleaning the air in the Central Valley.

Tax incentives, along with the lure of "free" fuel and the ability to sell the byproduct (electricity), caused an unprecedented building boom of biomass-fired power plants. Most of these plants were very small, so they were relatively quick to construct. In 1989, when we arrived in California, approximately 60 operating biomass power plants had produced 5,204,000 megawatt hours of electricity that year. It was an amazing boom of rampant construction and development.

While the premise of eliminating the open burn of millions upon millions of tons of organic waste was extremely smart and

El Nido Biomass Plant

viable, capitalism dictated that the "free" fuel quickly became a highly sought-after commodity. This was a game changer for many of the earlier developed, heavily debt-laden plants. This is where I came in at CAPCO.

I was supposed to study the process at the El Nido plant and figure out how to improve its efficiency enough to become profitable.

In fact, they would probably settle for breaking even. The El Nido Plant was only an 8 MW plant. It was a fluidized bed boiler using a steam turbine almost identical to the boiler feed pump turbines at the larger plants where I had worked earlier in my career. It was a total train wreck of design, functionality, and operability.

The only fuel available at an affordable price once this plant became operational was *garbage* no one else wanted. It consisted of cotton-gin trash and bottom-of-the-barrel yard waste that was mostly dirt and sand by the time it was delivered.

This so-called fuel was so low in heating value that it required massive amounts to produce the heat necessary for operation. This required fuel-feed rates to be substantially higher than designed to get enough heat to run the plant. This through-put eroded the boiler tubes in very short periods of time and caused boiler steam/water leaks. This, of course, required the plant to shut down for cooling and expensive repair.

The two El-Nido plant supervisors were young, recently discharged Navy veterans. Neither had seen a fluidized bed boiler prior to this. One of them, Bobby Castro, would become an employee and close friend many years down the road. He was extremely sharp but was currently working a job that was impossible to do.

After several weeks of extended hours at the El-Nido Plant, I submitted a sizable document to the "Brickhouse" containing my assessment of the plant. The Brickhouse was a converted home in Chowchilla, California, serving as the headquarters for CAPCO. There were very few people working there, and the major decision-maker was compromised on many different levels, a fact I had yet to learn. My voluminous report was easily condensed to this:

- **The fuel quality was wholly unusable in this (or any) plant.**
- **The plant had significant design flaws, each costing a substantial amount to correct.**
- **The plant was seriously understaffed.**
- **The provided budget was grossly insufficient, considering the accumulated and on-going maintenance costs.**

Harold Johnson was, as far as I knew, the primary CAPCO decision-maker. He was a tall, gray, bespectacled man in his early 50s with tight curly hair and a bushy, unkempt mustache smothering his upper lip. Every time I saw him, he was wearing the same buckskin-colored slacks and a green plaid shirt. I guess this was the only thing in his wardrobe. He was perpetually angry and usually shouting when he spoke. He was a very disgruntled man.

Upon submitting my lengthy report, he quickly skimmed through it while I sat in front of him. He angrily made it clear I was there to provide solutions for the existing situation and not to write reports explaining the *"obvious."*

Despite this, he asked me to begin work at their brand-new Madera Plant. It was a much larger plant (30 MW) and was constructed to utility standards. I didn't flinch at his request. It was about an hour away from our house in Merced, but it was a new, **substantially** nicer plant. We then drove to the Madera facility. The entire ride there was filled with him describing how nice the Madera plant was and how it was built to utility standards.

Upon arrival at the new plant, I found a unique situation. Construction was virtually complete, but the plant was not in start-up due to a fuel shortage. Harold provided a quick tour of the facility and then led me to the Plant Manager's office. He said that Ed Bowen, the Plant Manager, was on vacation for another week. Upon entering the nicely furnished, spacious office, Harold told me to have a seat.

I sat down in front of the Plant Manager's desk, and Harold sat behind the desk facing me. He then bluntly stated, "I need a decision from you *right now*."

Slightly taken aback, I pensively answered, "Okay, what is it I am supposed to decide?"

"I want you to take over as Plant Manager of this facility **_TODAY_** and work to bring this plant operational. We must produce power as soon as possible to create badly needed income."

I was shocked at his request. My mind took off in a hundred different directions. After a moment to reconcile his request, I answered.

"What am I supposed to do about fuel?"

"I WILL GET YOU SOME FUEL, DAMMIT!" He bellowed with anger. "It may be total shit, but it will be burnable, and **YOU MUST** make and sell some power with this facility as soon as possible so I can procure capital to keep this operation viable."

I struggled with everything I just heard. I knew I had to say something.

"What about staffing to run the plant?"

"This plant already has a minimal staff. You must adjust their hours to get the job done." He again raised his voice in anger. "Do you understand what I am saying? We must make some power. You are tasked with doing **whatever is necessary to get this done!**" His face was crimson red as he stared angrily at me. "Make your decision right now... *Do you want the Plant Manager position or not?*"

I thought about it for a moment. I had a multitude of questions but was worried about further stirring his anger by asking. However, I knew I had to ask the obvious question. "What does it pay, and what are the benefits?"

"Simple... You continue as a contractor, getting your pay and benefits from Burns and McDonnell Engineering. This way I can judge how well you handle the job, and you will still have a job if it doesn't work out here."

"So... Are we telling Burns and McDonnell about this?" I asked incredulously.

"I don't give a damn what you tell Burns and McDonnell. I need you to take over the management of this facility and give me some power. If it works out, we will hire you directly, and you will be here forever. If it doesn't, you will move on with them." He leaned forward and raised his arms with his hands outstretched. "What could be any simpler and beneficial to us all? Just take the damn job, and let's get this done!"

I thought for a moment (*obviously not enough*) and reached out my right hand. "I will do it." He vigorously shook my hand. After another more in-depth tour of the plant, he returned me to the Brickhouse to get my vehicle.

As I was leaving the Brickhouse, Harold walked to the driver's window of my car and leaned in. "I don't care how many hours you bill us. I don't care if you live at that plant 24 hours a day, 7 days a week. You make some power as soon as humanly possible. I will get fuel into the fuel yard in the next few days. You just make that plant run!"

The next four weeks, again, changed my life forever. I knew there were financial issues with CAPCO, but I had no idea that I just walked into a financial and political hornet's nest.

CHAPTER 10
THE MADERA FIASCO

Our lives had already been seriously compromised by my enormous, unbridled ego in Vernal Utah. I knew I could not allow any of the previous ego-errors to be repeated. I didn't realize until later that my ego had just convinced me to accept a job offer on the spot that was **blatantly** fraught with issues.

It was clear there were financial problems at CAPCO, but I never dreamed how bad they were. I also didn't consider the reason Harold didn't care how many hours I worked was because he had no intentions of paying Burns and McDonnell's invoices for my time.

I arrived at the plant very early the next morning and introduced myself to the two operators finishing the night shift. I told them I was the new Plant Manager. Their ambivalence was overwhelming, with the only noteworthy comment being, "Are you giving us a raise?"

After this anticlimactic encounter, I went to my new office to prepare for the first day. As the day shift personnel were arriving, I was confronted in my office by the plant Administrative Manager, Peggy. I was sitting at the Plant Manager's desk.

"Who are you?" She asked pensively as she poked her head into the office door.

I stood up from behind the desk and said, "I am Mark Gregg, the new Plant Manager."

Her voice immediately went from pensive to mildly irritated.

"What happened to Ed?"

"He's obviously been replaced." I was trying not to sound insolent, but I think it came off that way.

"Okaaaay…" Her countenance turned to skepticism. "I am Peggy, the Admin Manager. Why wasn't I told about this?"

"It just happened yesterday afternoon. I am sure Harold will be contacting you."

She thought for a moment before irately replying, "Would you be offended if I called Harold to confirm this?"

I immediately reached for the desk phone, poked the speaker button, and dialed Harold's office. It rang a few times before Harold answered. I was glad he answered. This encounter was already quite awkward.

"Johnson here." His voice was as gruff as always.

"Harold, Mark Gregg here. You are on the speaker. I am with Peggy, and she would like some confirmation that I am the new Plant Manager."

There was an odd, uncomfortable silence. Finally, he tersely stated, "Peggy, Mark's the new Plant Manager. You should put out a memo to that effect. I am busy and will call you later." The phone went dead. While I was now confirmed as the Plant Manager, it was even more awkward.

"Is he always that succinct?" I asked with a contrived smile, trying to reduce the uneasiness of the moment.

"He is definitely something... Her voice trailed off. "Yes, fine, I will do a memo. Do you want to approve it before I post it to the bulletin boards?" She made it very clear she was irritated.

"That would be great. Could you include the fact that I am going to be calling every employee into my office to meet them personally? Also, would you mind arranging for them to come to my office every 30 minutes or so today and tomorrow? I think it is very important that I meet everyone and introduce myself."

She glared at me and tersely replied, "*Fine*." As she turned and left. No questions, no chit-chat... *Nothing*.

It was an odd meeting. I knew something wasn't right with this whole situation. It was obvious she wasn't a fan of Harold, but I thought she would be a bit more welcoming. After all, we were going to be working together, right?

I spent the next two days meeting the minimally staffed plant. There were nine operators, two mechanics, one instrument technician, one electrician, and four fuel-handling personnel. The only other person on the payroll was Peggy. Eighteen total employees for a complex, 30 MW, fluidized bed boiler, biomass plant.

Meeting with the plant personnel painted a different picture than Harold painted. The plant had previously made a small amount of power. Harold failed to mention this *minor* fact. They used what little fuel they had and then shut down, waiting for more fuel. Apparently, during their short period of operation, the plant was problematic and experienced huge issues with high steam temperatures, baghouse issues, and an abundance of other problems. Nothing I heard was surprising for a new unit shakedown.

Ed Bowen, the previous plant manager, was painted as an older gentleman who was administratively minded and well-liked. The puzzle of me being made Plant Manager was even more confusing now than it was when Harold hired me.

The next week was spent on plant familiarization. I also was trying to determine the plant budget and the state of readiness for operation. The warehouse was, effectively, empty. The maintenance shop was pathetically equipped, and the water lab for the boiler was nothing more than a pH and conductivity monitor with some reagents to test for phosphate residuals. This was not even close to adequate for a high-pressure boiler. I mused that the water lab was not much better equipped than what you would require for a home swimming pool.

On Monday of the second week, an older, graying gentleman walked aggressively into my office. "Who the hell are you?" he asked indignantly.

I looked up from my desk. I had never seen this man before. "I am Mark Gregg, the Plant Manager. Who might you be?"

He looked angrily at me and said, "I am Ed Bowen, the *REAL* Plant Manager of this facility. How did you get access to my office?"

I was mortified. Ed Bowen? Why would he still believe *he* was the Plant Manager? *What is going on here…?* I then composed myself and slowly answered, "I was hired by CAPCO as the Plant Manager last week. I understood you were no longer employed here?" I made sure it was stated as a question.

His face turned violently angry. "This is total, complete bullshit." He shook his head several times. "I suppose it was that asshole Harold Johnson who did all this?"

"Yes, sir, it was," I replied slowly. I didn't know whether to apologize or hold my ground. To be honest, it was one of the most embarrassing moments of my career to this point. Making the moment worse was most of the feedback I received from the plant employees was positive towards this man. How could someone get treated this way? Until this moment, it appeared that he knew *nothing* of his termination or my hiring.

He walked straight over to my desk. I reared back a bit because I didn't know if he was going to assault me or shake my hand. He did neither. He violently grabbed the phone and dialed Harold's office. Harold answered. The conversation was quick and terse.

"Harold, this is Ed Bowen. I am standing in *MY f@%*& office* with what is apparently my replacement.

Would you mind telling me just what the hell is going on here?" I could tell Harold was yelling as usual, but couldn't quite make out what he was saying.

A moment later, the shouting on the other end of the phone stopped, and Ed yelled back, "Harold, you are a *&^%$* joke and a damn criminal. You **WILL** be hearing from my attorney!"

Ed slammed the phone down so hard I am surprised it didn't break and turned directly to me and put his finger in my chest. "Good luck, Craig, or whatever the hell your name is. You made the biggest mistake of your life coming to this train wreck." His demeanor then became belligerent, and mocking. "Are you aware that one of the CAPCO partners stole a ton of money and disappeared? Did dear Harold happen to mention this little factoid to you?" He paused, his face crimson red with anger. "Did you know they are not paying their bills?"

I stammered, "No, I was not aware of any of this."

"Well, you are now." He turned and walked towards the door, turning back towards me before he exited. "Where is all my personal shit?" He was looking around the office.

I pointed towards the door. "Peggy boxed everything last week. She has it in her office."

He spun around on his heels and finished walking out, slamming the door hard behind him. That was the last I ever saw or heard of Ed Bowen.

I was shaken to the core. I didn't know what to do. However, all the puzzle pieces were finally coming together. I didn't know whether to tell Vangie and upset her or just ride this one out. However, after thinking about it, I realized nothing had really changed. Harold himself said it when he "hired" me. I still worked for Burns and McDonnell Engineering. Harold could have me cleaning the restrooms, and I would still be paid a steady salary. If CAPCO didn't pay my invoice from Burns, they would have the option of moving me to another job. I decided to ride this one out and see what became of it. What else could I do at this point?

I called Steve Swain and told him to inform Burns and McDonnell personnel what was happening here and to see if he wanted me to remain. He said he was sure they were going to tell me to remain there as they had some kind of financial stake in the plant.

The next week, Harold delivered on his promise to provide fuel. It was primarily cotton-gin trash. This was the same material that was destroying El-Nido. Why cotton gin trash? Nothing to wonder about here. *No one else wanted it.* It was basically free for the hauling. It was primarily dirt and sand but contained some combustible material. Unfortunately, it became the basis of our fuel.

Oddly, some of the arriving fuel delivery trucks contained municipal construction waste. There was some highly prized wood in those shipments, but it was not screened or filtered. There were old tires, plain household garbage and other materials we were not allowed to burn, per our permit with the State of California. Harold was obviously doing some illegal things to get fuel.

100

Even worse, there were containers of medical waste. This was absolutely forbidden as it was supposed to be tracked. However, it was all destined to become fuel at this time. I knew then that Harold was quite compromised.

At least now, the fuel yard was starting to show some inventory. While it was mostly poor-quality material, I determined we finally had enough to start the plant. The early part of the start-up used natural gas for boiler bed warm-up. You could not start biomass feed until the fluidized bed was above 1200°, and you were generating steam. I decided that it was time to start putting systems into service and warming the boiler. I was given a mandate to make some electricity, and I was determined to accomplish this.

Across the road from the Madera plant was a Sun-Maid raisin's field covered with grapes that had been harvested and carefully laid out on the ground (albeit with some kind of cloth) to dry in the amazing California sun.

The name Sun-Maid was not just a moniker, it was truly how they made the raisins from grapes. I was amazed to see these huge vineyards with it's grapes just lying on the ground in the sun.

Unfortunately, the cotton gin trash and most of the other fuel we received created a tremendous amount of dust. *A stunning amount of eye-irritating, throat choking, dust.* The fuel yard was equipped with three very large dozers/loaders and two water trucks. The water trucks were critical, must-have, pieces of equipment necessary to suppress the dust.

Fugitive dust was considered and viewed by the state as being no different than particulate matter from the stack. We were required to keep fugitive dust to a minimum. This was a state mandate.

None of the rolling stock (heavy equipment) was in very good shape. It was all heavily used except for one of the water trucks. It was a newer unit and, according to my records, was leased. We were experiencing higher winds than usual, which required both water trucks to run consistently to keep the dust down.

My fourth week at the plant, the older, non-leased water truck's transmission failed. I immediately set the mechanics on getting it repaired. The next day the mechanics informed me that it required a new transmission. They also informed me that no one would extend credit for the transmission. I called Harold and told him what was happening.

Without warning, he exploded with a vulgar, expletive filled rant. He ended with, "YOU ARE THE @%$*! PLANT MANAGER... *FIGURE IT OUT*!"

That same afternoon, Jeff Gundy, a young man that appeared to be one of my best, and hardest working operators came into my office. He was quite agitated as he stated, "Mr. Gregg, my wife is being treated for cancer and the insurance company won't her bills. They say the insurance premiums from my employer have not been paid." He stopped for a moment and transitioned from being agitated to becoming emotional. "I pay part of that premium out of my check. Her bills are huge, but the treatment is keeping her alive… Do you know why they are saying the premiums aren't being paid?"

I was dumbfounded. I had no idea this was taking place. I picked up the phone and asked Peggy to come into my office.
She came in somewhat haltingly.

"Peggy, Jeff says that we are not paying his health insurance premiums. Do you know of an issue?"

Her eyes darted quickly between Jeff and me. With an air of total anxiety, she lowered her voice and said, "Let me look into this."

As soon as the words cleared her lips, she turned and left my office. I knew then something was wrong.

"Jeff, let us look into this. I give you my word I will get back to you shortly." He thanked me and left my office. As soon as he cleared the rear door of the admin building, Peggy bolted back into my office.

She seemed very disturbed. "We have not paid any health insurance premiums in over three months!" Her jaw then jutted in anger. "Harold said he was taking care of it. I haven't seen anything to lead me to believe that he has."

I shook my head in disbelief as I replied, "before his exit, Ed Bowen indicated to me that CAPCO's financial woes were caused by a shareholder or partner absconding with cash from the corporation. Do you know anything about this?"

She shrugged her shoulders. "I've heard rumors. I know that originally there were three primary partners, but now there are only two. Other than this, I don't know anything else for certain."

For the first time since I started there, she dropped her prickly demeanor and we talked for a bit. She admitted she was very concerned about the future of the company. I really couldn't console her because, frankly, I was also. Unfortunately, things began deteriorating very quickly from this point forward.

I now had to call Jeff back to my office and tell him we were trying to get to the bottom of the insurance premium issue. He broke down in my office and sobbed as he discussed his wife and her battle with cancer. He capped the conversation by pointing out he was now dealing with massive medical bills he couldn't afford to pay. I was helpless and empathetic but didn't have a clue what to do.

I called Harold, but he refused to discuss it. He just said, "I am working on it." It seemed any problem that he didn't have a solution for would resort to vulgarity and shouting, or saying he was working on it, or both. I now knew this place was going down.

In the fifth week, I was dealing with about 1000 technical issues with bringing the boiler online. I went back to my office to make a phone call to EPI, the boiler manufacturer when the wind began blowing exceptionally hard. The dust was seriously whipping up from the fuel yard.

As the wind accelerated, it began to look like a Middle Eastern Haboob, which was caused by the abundance of fuel

104

yard dust and dirt taking flight in the high winds. We couldn't keep the dust down with just one water truck, we needed at least two and maybe three water trucks to wet the fuel yard material enough to keep it on the ground.

Approximately 30 minutes later I received a call from a Sun-Maid representative saying if we didn't stop the fugitive dust emissions immediately, they were taking legal action against us. It seems the dust from our fuel yard haboob was covering their future raisins. Could it get any worse? *Yes, significantly.*

At 3:30 pm that day, two gentlemen from the equipment company that leased us the only running water truck arrived to repossess it. Apparently, we were several months behind in the lease payment. It was at that point I realized we were done. There was nothing I could do.

I surmised the immediate answer was to rig temporary PVC piping with sprinkler heads all over the fuel yard and pump water to them. A plan that would have worked, except we didn't have the piping, the pump, the sprinkler heads, or the time to put it together.

At about 5:00 pm, one of the mechanics returned from Fresno. He was trying to get parts for the bad transmission on the non-leased water truck. He came into my office out of breath and looking very concerned. He looked at me and said, "The Madera County APCD is up the road filming this place from a van. We are dusting really bad."

The APCD (Air Pollution Control District) is judge, jury, and trial. If they tell us to shut down the plant, you have no choice. It only took them about 45 more minutes to arrive in my office with a State Trooper.

I was given a written warning of exceedance and told I would be held responsible along with the CAPCO organization for what they termed *"the environmental disaster that was playing out."*

Once again, I reached a point in life where I was simply done. I tried calling Harold, but it was late enough I missed him. It was August of 1989, and there were no cell phones, so I immediately typed a letter of resignation and made it clear that I was terminating my contract on behalf of Burns and McDonnell. When completed, I signed and FAXED it to the Brickhouse.

Driving back to Merced, I was tormented with the thought that the captain was supposed to go down with the ship. I had to convince myself I wasn't a coward. I finally reasoned that I was NEVER really the Plant Manager. I still worked for Burns and McDonnell, and I certainly did not create this problem and certainly could not fix it.

I was convinced now that Harold was just trying to get some free labor. It was obvious he had no intention (or means) of ever paying Burns and McDonnell because it appeared no one else was getting paid.

When I arrived home that afternoon, I called my older brother Mike. He owned a car lot in Grand Junction, Colorado. I had shown him the Power Fundamentals course when we visited immediately prior to moving to Merced. At that time, he was impressed.

I decided this would be a perfect opportunity to pitch a partnership to him prior to calling Burns and McDonnell and telling them I needed another gig because this one was officially dead.

My phone call with Mike lasted well over an hour. We agreed to form a 50/50 partnership. I was to build the entire Power Fundamentals program, and he would market it when completed. He would supply our immediate financial needs and help us move to Grand Junction. He stressed that there would be no regular salary, just enough to keep the wolf from the door while I did the course development.

My single *non-negotiable* item was health insurance coverage. In 1989, Brandi was 13, Brittanie was 10, and Josh was 6 years old. I was adamant that we be put on his health insurance plan as we could not take the chance of having a serious health issue without the means to pay for it. *Jeff Gundy's situation was still fresh on my mind.*

He agreed.

We were now officially in business together. We didn't put anything on paper because we were brothers, and obviously, as brothers, we would never have any issues. While we did do a short, woefully inadequate contract down the road, it was too little, too late.

Vangie was intensely concerned about entering a partnership with family members. The moment I announced that Mike and I were starting this business together, she began fretting. She made it clear that going into business with family was a HUGE mistake, and she was against it.

107

Vangie felt we could figure out another way to do this without doing a partnership with a family member. I assured her it was going to be fine. I had no idea how accurate she was in her views. The upcoming issues came closer to tearing us apart than any other thing that ever happened in our marriage. Our journey was about to get exponentially more complex and would eventually play out far differently than any of us could see.

www.ingramcontent.com/pod-product-compliance
Lightning Source LLC
Chambersburg PA
CBHW061701120626
46550CB00003B/1037